D1049911

WORD, SOUND, AND IMAGE IN THE ODES OF HORACE

WORD, SOUND, AND IMAGE IN THE ODES OF HORACE

M. OWEN LEE

Ann Arbor
The University of Michigan Press

Library of Congress Catalog Card No. 69-15841
Published in the United States of America by
The University of Michigan Press and simultaneously
in Toronto, Canada, by Clarke, Irwin & Company Limited
Manufactured in the United States of America

Grateful acknowledgment is made to the following for permission to reprint material by the author which first appeared, in slightly different form, in the journals cited:

Classical Quarterly, for "Horace, *Odes* 1.4: A Sonic Circle," New Series 15 (1965), pp. 286-88. Oxford, The Clarendon Press.

Arion, for "Horace, *Odes* 1.11: The Lady Whose Name was Leu," 3 (1964), pp. 117-24. The University of Texas.

Classical Philology, for "Horace, *Carm.* 1.23: Simile and Metaphor," 60 (1965), pp. 185-86. The University of Chicago Press.

American Journal of Philology, for "Horace, *Odes* 1.38: Thirst For Life," 86 (1965), pp. 278-81. The Johns Hopkins Press.

CAUSA FUIT PATER HIS

PREFACE

The eminent position Horace still commands among the writers of the world is sufficient justification for yet another book on the Odes. Horace is a classic, and as such deserves not only respect but reassessment. "If he is a dubious classic, let us sift him; if he is a false classic, let us explode him. But if he is a real classic, if his work belongs to the class of the very best (for that is the true and right meaning of the word *classic, classical),* then the great thing for us is to feel and enjoy his work as deeply as ever we can."

This book is no sweeping reexamination of Horace. It neither sifts nor explodes. It does attempt what Matthew Arnold calls, plainly enough, "the great thing for us"; it attempts to deepen the feeling for and enjoyment of Horace's lyric art. This is no idle task. Arnold, commenting on the Greek and Latin instruction given in the schools almost a century ago, lamented that "the elaborate philological preparation goes on, but the authors are little known and less enjoyed." Today the elaborate philological machinery is grinding to a halt, and Horace in particular, because the Odes do not translate well, is read and enjoyed less than in the past, much less than he deserves. Yet he is a classic poet with surprisingly contemporary techniques. Students of poetry pass him over at their peril, lovers of the art, to their inestimable loss.

This book is addressed primarily to the undergraduates and secondary school teachers who asked for it, but it is hoped that anyone with some little Latin or less will be enabled hereby to see further into certain aspects (I like to think, important ones) of Horace's art and the art of poetry itself. To aid the literate but Latinless reader,

English translations are given where the sense of the Latin is not clear from the text.

A volume so slender as this can make no claim to be a complete survey, even of the poetic features which are its concern. The examples of Horatian hypallage, accommodation of sound to sense, associative imagery, etc. cited in chapters 2-4 of Part I are not meant to be exhaustive. They serve only to introduce various points used in the analyses that follow in Part II. The reader will discover for himself further instances of Horace's way with words and sounds and images.

The text used is the Oxford text of Wickham and Garrod (1959), differing only when a simplification (accusative plurals in *-es*) would expedite translation for the lay reader, or when a change of punctuation (1.11) or indentation (3.9) would facilitate reading.

I owe an immense debt to two books published in the last few years—Steele Commager's *The Odes of Horace* and L. P. Wilkinson's *Golden Latin Artistry*. Mr. Wilkinson, indeed, gave me personal attention and much encouragement. For this I am truly grateful. I should also like to thank *Classical Quarterly, Arion, Classical Philology,* and the *American Journal of Philology* for permission to reprint, in expanded form, the chapters on 1.4, 1.11, 1.23, and 1.38. A word of thanks is certainly due as well Professors G. B. Riddehough, W. B. Hennessey, W. E. McLeod, and Elisabeth McLeod, who read parts of the manuscript in preparation. Some of their cautions I have, perhaps unwisely, chosen to ignore; all criticism of the book must accordingly be directed toward the author alone. Finally I must thank the students who read Horace with me at St. Michael's College through the past five years; the elaborate philological preparation they brought to bear on the Odes helped me to know and love an author whose work, I am convinced, belongs to "the class of the very best."

CONTENTS

ABBREVIATIONS

AJP	*American Journal of Philology*
AP	*Ars Poetica*
CJ	*Classical Journal*
CP	*Classical Philology*
CQ	*Classical Quarterly*
CR	*Classical Review*
CS	*Carmen Saeculare*
CW	*Classical World*
GLA	L. P. Wilkinson, *Golden Latin Artistry* (Cambridge, 1963)
GR	*Greece and Rome*
HLP	L. P. Wilkinson, *Horace and His Lyric Poetry* (Cambridge, 1945)
HSCP	Harvard Studies in Classical Philology
LP	*Poetarum Lesbiorum Fragmenta,* ed. Edgar Lobel and Denys Page (Oxford, 1963)
P	*Poetae Melici Graeci,* ed. Denys Page (Oxford, 1962)
TAPA	Transactions of the American Philological Association
TCTIP	Gilbert Murray, *The Classical Tradition in Poetry* (Harvard, 1927)

PART I

An Introduction to Horace's Lyric Poetry

I

THE NOVELTY OF HORACE'S ODES

"Carmina non prius audita"

MORE THAN FIVE centuries lie between Alcaeus and Horace, and in that long interim Greeks and Romans wrote and read a good deal of poetry—elegies, pastorals, epics, epyllia—yet one feels there was nothing the Aeolian master, looking forward, or his Apulian disciple, looking back, would be compelled to call lyric. There were Hellenistic attempts to write in the old meters, but these were only curiosities—erudite, according-to-rule, emotionally exhausted. There was also Catullus, who had even fitted Latin words into the delicate lyric molds—but, so far as we know, only a few times. So when Horace placed before his public a whole collection of Latin poems in the five-hundred-year-old style and meters of Greek antiquity, he rightly claimed to be

> *princeps Aeolium carmen ad Italos*
> *deduxisse modos* (3.30.13-14).
>
> the first to have wed Greek song
> to Latin meters.

In the Rome of Horace's day the very idea of writing Greek lyrics in Latin must have seemed not so much irrelevant as impossible. Latin was heavier in sound and syntactically much less flexible than Greek, with more long syllables, fewer short monosyllables, and above all, speech rhythms formed by stress accent, not by pitch. It is true that Romans had learned, after years of practice, to write in a variety of Greek meters—those which allowed some metrical substitution. But Latin Sapphics and Asclepiads were almost unknown, and Latin Alcaics were unheard of—until 23 B.C., when Horace published the first three books of the Odes: eighty-eight compact, highly finished poems in the intricate rhythmic patterns of *Lyra Graeca,* fashioned entirely from virile, sonorous and hitherto intractable Latin words. Though the first public reaction was disappointing, Horace eventually became a classic in his own day, and in 13 B.C. he added fifteen additional Odes as Book IV.

With this collection of lyrics, Horace made three contributions of considerable importance for poets of succeeding centuries (poets of his own day seem to have been too overawed to follow him). The first of these is the restoration of the stanza[1] to its proper place in lyric art. In the five centuries separating Horace from Alcaeus and the Greek lyricists, the only stanzaic verse we know are four poems of Catullus; the rest was repetition of a single metrical line or at most the couplet. After Horace, through Hilary, Villon, and Petrarch to Herrick, Eichendorff, and Robert Frost, we have had, overwhelmingly, lyric poetry in stanzas. We have consistently regarded the stanza as the natural vehicle for lyric expression.

Secondly, Horace experimented with new and bold arrangements of words. The word order in Latin verse had always differed from that of prose: while Cicero was writing majestic prose periods that moved inexorably toward their anchoring verbs, Lucretius proved that a line of poetry gained considerably in force if the verb could be placed between noun and adjective, and in the longer poems of Catullus this separation of grammatically related words became almost de rigueur. But Horace was the first to extend this verse order throughout a four-line stanza and even past the stanzaic framework. He arranged words in patterns as elaborate as any by his Greek masters, and in the process showed that the juxtaposition of grammatically unrelated words could suggest new levels of meaning unknown to prose (and impossible in uninflected languages). More than any previous Latin poet, he experimented with the interplay of literal and suggested meanings in his carefully placed words.

The third notable feature in Horace is what I would call the associative flow of images through most if not all of the Odes. This may seem to be reading contemporary method into classic verse, but the allusive use of symbols was not unknown in antiquity, and may in fact be essential to the construction of odes, as Norwood suggests in the case of Pindar.[2] Horace's images fall into predictable and significant groupings, and sometimes a poem's structure or relevance or even literal meaning can be satisfactorily explained only by examining the pattern of its imagery. For the Odes of Horace are neither lyrical effusions nor plain statements of fact. They say what they must concisely, for the most part dispassionately, and above all obliquely, through myth and symbol, implication and association. They are charged with more than one variety of Empson's ambiguity. They are, in a word, *contemporary* classics. Janus-like, Horace looks back to Alcaeus and forward to our own present-day poets—and no doubt past them.

Criticism of Horace has usually centered on alleged deficiencies: he lacks imagination, descriptive power, emotional force, true sentiment, profundity of thought, good taste in choice of subject matter, spontaneity. I like to think that Horace has all these qualities in good, if not always in abundant, supply and that any fault lies not with him but with his critics. It is not a question of Horace having to sacrifice these values to maintain his own exacting technical standards. Rather, we have been so absorbed by the surface polish of his performance that we have failed to see underlying values of a less technical nature. We have been drilled in the Odes and have got them by heart. They hardly impress us as poetry at all, and their author seems a genial phrase-maker, a highly skilled craftsman, little more. Until recently, we had similar difficulty appreciating Mozart, another artist with astounding technical skill and high standards of perfection. The classic poet and the eighteenth-century composer may be profitably compared. Both arrange their experience in formal patterns; both specialize in the tour de force of technique, the deft surprise, the stylized expression of firmly controlled but often intense emotion. The very precision of their art enables them to achieve, with seeming ease, small miracles of expressiveness which may completely escape the notice of the casual or unsympathetic observer. We, not they, are the poorer if we cannot see strength in their delicacy, imagination and originality in their use of form, depth of meaning beneath their surface brilliance.

Of course, Horace never claimed to be imaginative or tasteful or touching or profound. He only claimed to be first and best at wedding his own Italian speech to the lyrics of a vibrant civilization far distant in time and space. We are to judge him, if we must, on this basis: Latin words and Greek rhythms. It is the purpose of this book to examine Horace's use of words, sounds, and images. If we look to these, we may find as well the values we have perennially missed in this Roman innovator par excellence.

2

WORDS

"Beauty of form has made him immortal, and fully half that beauty lies in the order of his words."

—Gilbert Murray

Poems are made from words. But not quite as walls are made from bricks. Bricks are durable and insensitive. They are, moreover, made for building. But words—some simply do not look right on the printed page; others are not suited to the metrical scheme; others are too lofty or too lowly for the poet's purpose:

> *audebit, quaecumque parum splendoris habebunt*
> *et sine pondere erunt et honore indigna ferentur,*
> *verba movere loco, quamvis invita recedant*
> (*Epistles 2.2.111-13*).

> (The poet) will have the courage to strike out all such words as have not the requisite beauty, gravity or dignity, though they may not want to give place.[1]

If nothing else will do, picturesque archaisms will have to be called forth from retirement:

> *obscurata diu populo bonus eruet atque*
> *proferet in lucem speciosa vocabula rerum,*
> *quae priscis memorata Catonibus atque Cethegis*
> *nunc situs informis premit et deserta vetustas*
> (115-19).

> Words long buried in darkness the good poet will unearth and bring to light—those picturesque phrases which were once mouthed by old Cato and Cethegus and the rest, but which have grown old and ugly and are now covered over with the rust of neglect.

Occasionally, and with great care, new words can be forged:

> *si forte necesse est*
> *indiciis monstrare recentibus abdita rerum,*
> *fingere cinctutis non exaudita Cethegis*
> *continget, dabiturque licentia sumpta pudenter*
> (*AP* 48-51).

> If it so happens that you need new terms to explain some abstruse subject, then you have a proper occasion to coin words never heard by the straight-laced Cethegi; the right will be yours, if you use it with restraint.

But a careful and sensitive poet will not need to resort to extreme measures often. He will use old words and give them new luster by juxtaposition:

> *in verbis etiam tenuis cautusque serendis*
> *dixeris egregie notum si callida verbum*
> *reddiderit iunctura novum* (46-48).

> Be sensitive, too, and careful in combining words. You will have spoken especially well, if some clever juxtaposition has made a familiar word new.

In this last department Horace has set a standard still unequalled by the world's poets. The *callida iunctura* is his specialty. Of all the accolades accorded it, Nietzsche's, the most quoted, is still the most apt:

> This mosaic of words, in which every word, by sound, by position and by meaning, diffuses its influence to right and left and over the whole.[2]

The reader may think "every word" at least a slight exaggeration,[3] but there are poets who will not think it so. T. S. Eliot sees in poetry a "perpetual slight alteration of language, words perpetually juxtaposed in new and sudden combinations."[4] In a poem, as in a sentence,

> every word is at home,
> Taking its place to support the others,
> The word neither diffident nor ostentatious,
> An easy commerce of the old and the new,
> The common word exact without vulgarity,
> The formal word precise but not pedantic,
> The complete consort dancing together.[5]

On the simplest level, Horace is unequalled in the placing of words for eye-catching effect in the stanza. And while Nietzsche may see them as tiny pieces of a mosaic, blocks or hewn stones might be a more apt description for the words as structured in almost any of Horace's Sapphic stanzas:

> *rebus angustis animosus atque*
> *fortis appare; sapienter idem*
> *contrahes vento nimium secundo*
> *turgida vela* (2.10.21-24).

Here is a metrical scheme modeled on the light stanza of a Greek poetess but reworked[6] so as to give maximum effect to great resounding Latin words built into some sort of lapidary statement. The words seem to fall by their own weight into place, leaving at the close a single dactyl and spondee, visually isolated and musically resounding, lodged in the memory.

Another stanza from the same poem will show how the ode's theme—the Golden Mean—is emphasized by the placing of the key word, the double-weighted *mediocritatem,* above the neatly substructured phrases *caret obsoleti* and *caret invidenda*:

auream quisquis mediocritatem
diligit, tutus caret obsoleti
sordibus tecti, caret invidenda
sobrius aula (5-8).

If the eye is allowed to move vertically through the stanza, the reader sees as well as hears the echoes: *quisquis . . . tutus . . . tecti*; *sordibus . . . sobrius*. Part of the credit for these effects must go to the Latin language, which dispenses with the article, auxiliary verbs, and many prepositions—smaller words which might tend to clutter the line. (The necessary monosyllables, *si* and *non* and the rest, can be worked into a line of poetry unobtrusively: in the poem from which we have quoted, all but two of these are concentrated in a single stanza.) But most of the credit must go to Horace, who strives to give each word an importance, a visual, almost tactile role in the structure of the stanza.

Because Latin is an inflected language, the endings of the words will establish the necessary grammatical relationships, and there is no need, as in modern languages, to place the words in an order demanded by the sense. Words can be rearranged almost at will, and to striking effect. In the first ode of Horace, a Marsian boar is, on the printed page, within the supple nets:

teretes Marsus aper plagas (1.1.28),

a hind is sighted, and surrounded, by faithful hounds:

catulis cerva fidelibus (27),

and a peaceful gentleman's limbs are quite visually shaded by a green arbutus:

viridi membra sub arbuto (21).

Similarly, Horace illustrates how sea-monsters fill the teeming ocean:

scatentem / beluis pontum (3.27.26-27),

how Bandusia's oak is set amid hollow rocks:

cavis impositam ilicem / saxis (3.13.14-15),

how, within the thick cloud which rescued him from Philippi, he did the trembling, Mercury the lifting:

denso paventem sustulit aëre (2.7.14).

There are examples of this by the hundred, but the *locus classicus* for such word-placing is the fifth ode in the first book. The lady addressed is embraced by a handsome boy:

gracilis te puer,

and the two are surrounded by roses:

multa gracilis te puer in rosa (1.5.1).

It seems the lady, Pyrrha, lies within a pleasure cave:

grato, Pyrrha, sub antro (3)

by the side of a sea tossed by black winds:

nigris aequora ventis (7).

The boy and girl embrace:

qui nunc te fruitur credulus aurea (9),

while Horace, thankful for his escape from this siren, puts up a votive plaque on a chapel wall, with his dripping garments as testimonial, to the powerful sea-god who effected his rescue—and the nouns and adjectives, arranged in interlocking pairs before and after the main verb, form a checkerwork as intricate as the plaque-covered chapel wall itself:

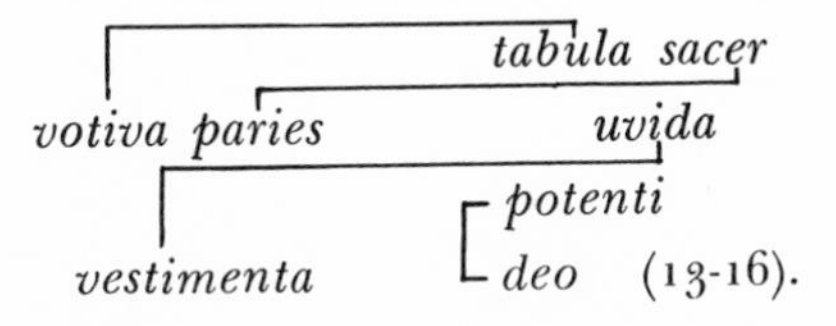

This effect has only recently been marked by writers on Horace[7]—though one suspects that the schoolboy, numbering the words in order in his text, saw it long ago.

Traditional Patterns

A word-pattern favored by ancient grammarians is *chiasmus,* wherein corresponding pairs of words are arranged so as to form the letter chi (x) if one pair is written above the other:

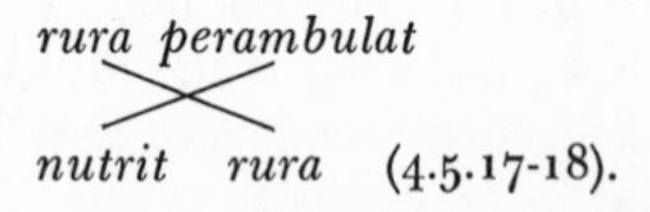

Horace does not make extensive use of this somewhat rhetorical device. But more than two dozen times in the Odes we find the so-called Golden Verse, defined by Dryden as "two substantives and two adjectives with a verb betwixt to keep the peace."[8] In Horace the two adjectives almost invariably come first, and the resulting arrangement is sometimes chiastic:

> *fragilem truci / commisit pelago ratem* (1.3.10-11),

sometimes achiastic, or interlocking:

> *superiecto pavidae natarunt / aequore dammae*
> (1.2.11-12).[9]

The effect is to afford the reader a glimpse first of the detail, descriptive or emotional, leaving subject matter undefined until the verb has, as it were, brought the picture to life, e.g.:

> a fragile–to the savage–he entrusted–to the sea–
> a skiff,

and:

> in the overwhelming–trembling–they swam–
> in the water–deer.

Shared Epithet

Often Horace intends a single adjective to qualify two nouns, and accordingly places it between the two (though it is conjoined only to the second). Thus the lad making love to Pyrrha will often bewail her (broken) promise and the fickle gods:

fidem / mutatosque deos flebit (1.5.5-6).

Both the horses and the chariot of the sky-god are winged:

equos volucremque currum (1.34.8).

Both senate and traditional values are subverted by the defection of Crassus' soldiers:

pro curia inversique mores (3.5.7).[10]

Similarly, a well placed adjective can serve adverbially to qualify two verbs. Both Horace and his serving boy are *sedulus*:

nihil allabores / sedulus curo (1.38.5-6).

I earnestly ask that you add
nothing, in your earnestness.

Transferred Epithet

Horace is fond of the figure of speech known as hypallage or transferred epithet: an adjective appearing in a context with two substantives seems to have been transferred from the one to which it belongs in sense, and made to agree grammatically with the other. The reader is jolted, recognizes the figure, pauses to transfer the epithet back to its proper substantive, while marking that, in a secondary sense at least, it does somehow qualify the word it is made to modify. So Queen Cleopatra is said to prepare "mad ruin" for the Capitol:

regina dementes ruinas (1.37.7).

Surely, one thinks, the *dementes* should be *demens,* modifying *regina*: she is spoken of as maddened and deranged throughout the first half of the poem, and transferring the epithet gives the passage a neat parallelism—"the mad queen was plotting ruin for the Capitol and destruction for the empire." But as the words stand the effect is richer: *dementes* between the two similar-sounding nouns goes in sense with *regina* and grammatically (and in a secondary sense, and with graphic effect) with *ruinas*.

When he uses this figure, Horace usually contrives to juxtapose the epithet and the word with which it goes in sense. So we do not allow angry Jove to lay aside his (angry) thunderbolts:

*iracund*a *Iovem ponere fulmin*a (1.3.40),

and glistening Minos passes (glistening) judgment:

*splendid*a *Minos / fecerit arbitri*a (4.7.21-22),

and the poet came close to seeing the dusky realms of (dusky) Proserpine:

*furv*ae *regna Proserpin*ae (2.13.21).[11]

Richer and more startling still are the instances of *double* hypallage. In Horace's opening poem, the peaceful man is said to recline at times at the gentle source of some sacred stream:

ad aquae lene caput sacrae (1.1.22).

But, we reflect, the guardian nymph dwells at the *source* of the stream: *sacrae* should modify *caput*. And the stream would hardly be one to rest by unless its *waters* were gently rippling: *lene* should modify *aquae*. The complex, magical phrase is usually translated with both epithets transferred, "at the sacred source of some gentle stream," but any translation must lose fully half of the original. And again, Horace's placing of the words has helped.

Another fine example of double hypallage is in the ode to Pyrrha:

aspera / nigris aequora ventis (1.5.6-7).

Does this mean "the sea roughened by dark winds" or "the sea darkened by rough winds"? To the reader's delight and the translator's despair, it means both.

Double hypallage is the best solution to the riddle posed by Horace's famous boast:

princeps Aeolium carmen ad Italos
deduxisse modos (3.30.13-14).

Surely, the puzzled reader objects, this is not right; Horace brought Latin song to Greek meters, not vice versa. But when both epithets are transferred,[12] the boast is well founded: Horace was the first to bring Latin song to Greek (at least, if we except three poems by Catullus, to Aeolian) meters. Then, knowing Horace's way with hypallage, we pause to look into the secondary sense, and note that the expression is, even as it stands, quite true, and a part of Horace's glorious claim: his Latin *carmen* has a Greek delicacy and finish, and the *modi* originated by Greeks will ever after be thought of as Latin—indeed, as Horatian.

Hendiadys

On an equal level of invention is Horace's use of hendiadys —the expression of a single idea by two connected nouns. Invariably the second of the two qualifies the first, adding the personal, the graphic, the limiting detail. So when Horace reminds Pompeius how they experienced the swift rout at Philippi:

Philippos et celerem fugam (2.7.9),

what he says in effect is "with you I experienced Philippi— (not the glory of it, but) the unceremonious retreat." So an enormous troop of impious Titans:

impios / Titanas immanemque turbam (3.4.42-43)

is, more properly, "impious Titans—a great swarm of them." And mists and bad weather:

nebulae malusque / Iuppiter (1.22.19-20)

are "mists—the kind Jupiter sends when he is in a bad mood."

There is a pair of such expressions (and another *celerem fugam*) in 2.13.17-19:

> *miles sagittas et celerem fugam*
> *Parthi, catenas Parthus et Italum*
> *robur . . .*

The full implication here is that the (Roman) soldier fears arrows—(not just any arrows, but) those the Parthians shoot on their swift retreat-maneuver, while the Parthian fears imprisonment—(not at home, but) in the Roman strong-place in the Mamertine.

Oxymoron

The ancient species of paradox known as oxymoron is only a sophisticated use of word-placing, and Horace is the prime exponent of this sort of literary jolt. Hypermnestra, who alone of Danaus' fifty daughters disobeyed paternal orders and spared her husband on that fatal wedding night, is gloriously deceitful (*splendide mendax* 3.11.35); Juba's land is dry, but it nurses lions (*leonum / arida nutrix* 1.22.15-16); the wine jug wrests secrets from the tippler, so it may be called a gentle sort of rack (*lene tormentum* 3.21.13). Less famous than these examples, but worth noting, are the reference to the mad wisdom of Epicurean thought (*insanientis . . . sapientiae* 1.34.2—usually overlooked in the discussion of Lucretius' reported madness), and that egregious pun—Regulus hastening forth to exile an *egregius . . . exsul* (3.5.48), i.e., not only glorious but, in exile, standing out from the *grex*.

Most of the punning in Horace's Odes owes at least as much to word-placing as it does to verbal similarities. Mercury is *lyrae parentem* (1.10.6), though in the context we are reminded that he was a *puer* (actually not a full day old) when he fathered the lyre; the Argonauts looked undismayed at the terrors of the sea, but as the words and their placing have it, they looked with dry eyes at swimming monsters:

siccis oculis monstra natantia (1.3.18).

At times, the juxtaposition of proper name and qualifying pun is wit of the subtlest variety, defying translation:

Parca non mendax (2.16.39)

the sparing goddess, true to her name

immitis Glycerae (1.33.2)

your embittered Sweetheart

Lalagen . . . dulce loquentem (1.22.23-24)

my sweet-talking Chatterbox

Bibuli consulis amphoram (3.28.8)

a wine jar from Bibulus' consulship.

Association

As words carry the weight of associations, a strategically placed word can call up the memory of a separate context. Thus, memories of Homer may be evoked by such brief phrases as *densentur funera* (1.28.19—cf. Homer's αἰεὶ δὲ πυραὶ νεκύων καίοντο θαμεῖαι in *Iliad* 1.52), and *iuga demeret/ bobus* (3.6.42-43—cf. Homer's recurrent βουλυτόνδε), and *quicumque terrae munere vescimur* (2.14.10—cf. Homer's βροτῶν, οἳ ἀρούρης καρπὸν ἔδουσιν in *Iliad* 6.142, and ὅσσοι νῦν βροτοί εἰσιν ἐπὶ χθονὶ σῖτον ἔδοντες in *Odyssey* 8.222). But Horace's personal experience is bound up less with Homer than with the lyric poets of Greece:

non, si priores Maeonius tenet
sedes Homerus, Pindaricae latent
Ceaeque et Alcaei minaces
Stesichorive graves Camenae;

nec, si quid olim lusit Anacreon,
delevit aetas; spirat adhuc amor
vivuntque commissi calores
Aeoliae fidibus puellae

(4.9.5-12).

> Even though Maeonian Homer holds first place, the other muses do not hide their faces—not Pindar's, or Simonides', or Alcaeus' warlike maid, or the stately muse of Stesichorus;
>
> nor has time destroyed all that Anacreon wrote in sport; and that love still breathes, those passions still live that were confided to the harp-strings of the Aeolian maid.

Horace borrowed themes as well as meters from these predecessors, particularly from Alcaeus. The devotion of Roman disciple to Greek master is revealed twice, in the touching 1.32 and the semi-humorous 2.13. At least a few of the Odes are free and imaginative adaptations of Alcaean poems: the hymn to Mercury, 1.10, may be compared with fragment 308 LP, and the "ship of state" ode, 1.14, with fragment 326 LP.

Adaptations, however, were not Horace's real purpose. He rather employs quotations from the Greek lyricists as motifs in the Odes—a not inappropriate device for a poet who was apprenticed to these writers, and almost obsessively desirous of joining their ranks. Latinized bits of *Lyra Graeca* thread their way through the Odes, charged no doubt with personal associations for Horace himself, imbuing his poems with a romantic, centuries-old atmosphere, and challenging the educated reader to intellectual as well as emotional response. Though we cannot hope to trace all of Horace's allusive borrowings from the now fragmentary writings of Alcaeus, we can see, for example, that the opening of the Cleopatra ode (*Nunc est bibendum,* 1.37) is a Latinized quote from Alcaeus' celebration of the fall of the Lesbian tyrant Myrsilus (332 LP), that 1.9 (the Soracte ode), 1.18, and 3.12 all take their opening "mottoes" from once-familiar lyrics of Alcaeus (338, 342, and 10 LP) and then veer off on new poetic tangents; that Simonides is probably the source of the famous *innumerabilis / annorum series et fuga temporum* (3.30.4-5); that there are echoes of Anacreon in 1.23, the ode to Chloë as fawn (408 P), in 1.27, the brawl over the drinking cups (356 P), in 1.25, 2.5, and 3.11; that 1.12 begins with a Pindaric "motto" and is reminiscent throughout of the second Olympian; that 1.15 is modeled on Bacchylides. As Pasquali[13] is at pains to point out, this is not *imitatio.* It is an allusive and very personal use of literature and its associations. One is reminded of T. S. Eliot's elaborate deployment of passages from the many writers who people his subconscious.[14]

To a lesser extent, Latin poets are quoted for effect. When Horace writes an ode for Virgil, he pays him the compliment of using words Virgil has charged with meaning. The third ode in the first book, addressed to the ship bearing Virgil on a perilous voyage, contains a number of references to and words from the sea-scenes in the early books of the *Aeneid.* Aeolus and his prison of the winds, Africus, Notus, Aquilo, and the Hyades are all transferred from Aeneas' Mediterranean to the sea which Virgil must cross and which is for Horace almost symbolic of destruction, the Adriatic. A Virgilian line:

> *et mulcere dedit fluctus et tollere vento* (1.66)
>
> and gave the power to soothe the waves, and lift
> them with the wind

prompts the Horatian:

> *tollere seu ponere volt freta* (1.3.16)
>
> whether he choose to lift or lull the
> sea.

But most notable in both poets is the use of *incubo.* Properly the word means "lie upon," but in the sea passages of the first books of the *Aeneid*[15] Virgil gives it an ominous, sinister force; it comes to mean "brood over, settle upon." So when the word appears in Horace's ode on Virgil's sea voyage:

> *et nova febrium*
> *terris incubuit cohors* (1.3.30-31)
> and a legion of strange diseases
> settled upon the earth,

we think of the *febres* as malevolent powers settling like birds of ill omen upon their victim.

The spirit of Catullus is invoked in 1.22, which virtually quotes both of the earlier poet's efforts in the Sapphic meter: *iter . . . facturus* (1.22.5-6) with attendant travelogue is close to the opening of Catullus 11, while *dulce ridentem* (1.22.23) is an unmistakable quotation from Catullus 51. Also reminiscent of Catullus 11 is Horace 2.6: though the earlier poem is full of half-smothered sarcasm and the latter is genial and sentimental, both begin with a *vade-mecum* and end with unexpected poignancy; Horace even recalls Catullus' best adonic (*tunditur unda*) with his similarly placed *aestuat unda*. Then Horace's Lydia is much like Catullus' Lesbia: she causes the poet's senses to quiver and quake (compare Catullus 51 and Horace 1.13); she enters into amoebean discourse with him (compare Catullus 45 and Horace 3.9); and Lydia, it is forecast, will end her days as Catullus says Lesbia did, a tramp in a narrow alleyway, *in solo levis angiportu* (Horace 1.25.10—compare Catullus 58 and the use of *levis* in 72.6). Finally Horace begins the last of his spring songs with a tribute to Catullus: *iam veris comites* (Horace 4.12.1—compare Catullus 46.1, 9), and then writes a variant of Catullus 13: Virgil is invited to dinner but must bring his own ointment. In each case it is the carefully chosen, carefully placed word which brings the association of the previous context to bear on the present one. Catullus himself is never mentioned.

Nor is Lucretius, but similar compliments are nonetheless paid him, particularly in the odes of Book II, with its predominantly Epicurean tone.[16] Lucretius' line

iam iam non domus accipiet te laeta, neque uxor
(3.894)

no more, no more will your happy home welcome
you, nor your wife

is the source of Horace's

linquenda tellus et domus et placens / uxor
(2.14.21-22).

you must leave your land and home and loving wife.[17]

The opening stanzas of 2.16 (*Otium divos*) may recall Catullus' Sapphic stanza on *otium,* but there is a distinct echo of Lucretius as well in the lines:

patriae quis exsul
se quoque fugit? (19-20)

what man, exiled from his country,
escapes himself as well?

Lucretius has *hoc se quoque modo fugit* (3.1068), and similarly in a section where he describes the vain attempts of men to escape anxieties that gnaw from within. Finally, in the loveliest of the spring songs, Horace begins with a stanza which may call to mind the opening of Lucretius' poem:

Diffugere nives, redeunt iam gramina campis
arboribusque comae;
mutat terra vices, et decrescentia ripas
flumina praetereunt (4.7.1-4).

The snows have fled. So soon the grass is come
back to the fields, the leaves to the trees.
The earth is changing its seasons, and subsiding
rivers are flowing past their banks.[18]

The third stanza seems a reworking of Lucretius' parade of the seasons in Book v:

frigora mitescunt Zephyris, ver proterit aestas
interitura simul
pomifer autumnus fruges effuderit, et mox
bruma recurrit iners (9-12).

Winter gives way to Spring's breath, Summer drives away Spring, only to perish itself as soon as apple-bearing Autumn has poured forth its fruits. And soon Winter stumbles back, all-but-dead.[19]

With Horace's next stanza, the echoes are surer and remarkably varied:

damna tamen celeres reparant caelestia lunae:
nos, ubi decidimus
quo pater Aeneas, quo Tullus dives et Ancus,
pulvis et umbra sumus (13-16).

Yet the swift-changing moon repairs its heavenly losses. We, when once we have descended whither father Aeneas and king Tullus and Ancus have gone, we are dust and shadow.

Line 15 is reminiscent of Virgil (*pater Aeneas*), of Horace's *Epistles* (1.6.27), of Lucretius:

lumina sis oculis etiam bonus Ancus reliquit
(3.1025)

even good Ancus closed his eyes to the light of day,

and of the passage Lucretius was using from Ennius (*Annals* 149). And the evocative line is set in a paraphrase of Catullus'

soles occidere et redire possunt:
nobis, cum semel occidit brevis lux,
nox est perpetua una dormienda
(5.4-6).

The sun can set and rise again.
But for us, when once our brief light
  has set,
there is but one everlasting night to
  sleep through.

nobis, cum semel occidit:: *nos, ubi decidimus*—Horace's words have special poignancy when we set them against those of the earlier poet. The theme has changed from major to minor: Catullus' *soles* become *lunae* in Horace; peaceful, everlasting night has turned to dust and shadow; Catullus' regular hendecasyllables are part of a vigorous affirmation of life, while Horace's uneven distichs are resigned and melancholy—every second line is halted, almost hushed.

As for associative use of his own work, Horace sometimes refashions whole odes (1.4 and 4.7 are variations on the same theme, as are 2.3 and 2.14), but usually it is only a slight touch, a combination of words, that calls to mind an association elsewhere. Why is the last stanza of the ode to the *fons Bandusiae* so charming? If those melodious lines:

fies nobilium tu quoque fontium,
me dicente cavis impositam ilicem
  saxis, unde loquaces
    lymphae desiliunt tuae (3.13.13-16),

You too will become one of those glorious fountains, as I sing of the oak tree perched on hollow rocks, whence your speaking waters leap down,

are compared with a couplet from the Epodes:

mella cava manant ex ilice, montibus altis
  levis crepante lympha desilit pede (16.47-48),

Honey flows from the hollow oak tree, and from the steep hills gentle water leaps down with splashing step, it will be seen that not only the phrase *lymphae desiliunt* but *cavis . . . ilicem* as well carries liquid association for Horace, and for the reader who is alert to the word-placing.

Callida Iunctura

We have mentioned thus far word-placing of various types for various effects, but have yet to touch upon the heart of the matter—what Horace himself styled *callida iunctura,* and Gilbert Murray described as "juxtaposition of those words which specially affect or explain or intensify one another, and so, without altering the intellectual meaning of the sentence, invest it with depths and shades of feeling, and knit it into a whole, like Aristotle's 'live animal.' "[20] It is largely because commentators and critics, even the best of them, were insensitive to Horace's *iuncturae* that some of the famous odes have been slighted as incoherent, "sad stuff" or "poor" or "vile" or "trash."[21]

First, it should be said again (and Horace never tires of saying it in his critical writings)[22] that words have a life of their own; they have ancestors, a place of birth (which can often be traced), and as they live out their life-spans they take on associations more or less personal to themselves. The poet specializes in these associations—the overtones, the connotations, the suggestive power in words. In poetry, as Cleanth Brooks puts it, "the connotations play as great a part as the denotations."[23] Therein lies the difference between the scientist and the poet in their use of language: science uses the denotations, restricting the meanings of words to their dictionary definitions; poetry cannot ignore the denotations, but must also be sensitive to the connotations of words. Indeed, in so doing, it sometimes expands and explodes the dictionary meanings. Why do we need art at all if not for this? Art expresses what science, with its self-imposed principles of investigation, never can. Think of the sea as a chemical formula or as the subject of the science of oceanography—and then think what it means to Conrad, Turner, and Debussy. Think of sorrow as a psychological phenomenon or as a physical disturbance—and then think how Mozart expressed it in his G Minor symphony. Art seems to exist to give expression to vast areas of non-conceptual knowledge, feeling and association which the more reasoned, impersonal fields of philosophy and science cannot express.

Was Horace sensitive to the overtones in words? Let us look again at that passage from the *Ars Poetica.*

> *in verbis etiam tenuis cautusque serendis*
> *dixeris egregie notum si callida verbum*
> *reddiderit iunctura novum* (46-48).

Callida iunctura—two well-worn words carefully juxtaposed can take on new meanings. Each word, to quote Brooks again, "has to be conceived of, not as a discrete particle of meaning, but as a potential of meaning, a nexus or cluster of meanings."[24]

The most striking single instance[25] of this in Horace's Odes (striking in itself and also because it has enabled "new critics" to defend the poem from its attackers) is the two-word phrase lodged in the middle of the seemingly disjointed Soracte ode:

> *virenti canities* (1.9.17).

The lexicon meanings of the two words are "vigorous" and "a whitish-grey color." But when the two words are juxtaposed, *virenti* (vigorous) reminds the reader that *canities* can also stand for "old age," and *canities* (white) in turn colors *virenti*: we recall that it can legitimately mean "green." Here, at least, Nietzsche was right. Each word "diffuses its influence to the right and left," so that the other takes on an additional meaning. But more astonishing is how their influence extends "over the whole":

> *Vides ut alta stet nive candidum*
> *Soracte, nec iam sustineant onus*
> *silvae laborantes, geluque*
> *flumina constiterint acuto.*

dissolve frigus ligna super foco
large reponens atque benignius
deprome quadrimum Sabina,
o Thaliarche, merum diota.

permitte divis cetera, qui simul
stravere ventos aequore fervido
deproeliantes, nec cupressi
nec veteres agitantur orni.

quid sit futurum cras fuge quaerere et
quem Fors dierum cumque dabit lucro
appone, nec dulces amores
sperne puer neque tu choreas,

donec virenti canities abest
morosa. nunc et campus et areae
lenesque sub noctem susurri
composita repetantur hora,

nunc et latentis proditor intimo
gratus puellae risus ab angulo
pignusque dereptum lacertis
aut digito male pertinaci.

You see how Soracte stands shimmering in deep snow, how the straining woods no longer support their burden, how the rivers are halted by the sharp ice.

Take the chill off, pile the logs high on the hearth, Thaliarchus, and draw more generous draughts of four-year wine from the Sabine jar.

Leave the rest to the gods, for once they have laid to rest the winds that clash in battle on the raging sea, no cypress, no venerable ash tree stirs.

Ask not what the morrow will bring. Put down as gain each day that fate grants

> you. And spurn not the delights of love and the dance, my boy,
>
> As long as hoary old age lingers afar from your green youth. Now is the time to seek out the Campus Martius and the city squares, and soft whispering in the night at the trysting hour.
>
> Now is the time for happy laughter from some secret corner (betraying the lass hiding there), and a token wrested from an arm or finger that scarcely resists at all.

Until recently, this poem has been criticized[26] as lacking that very unity Horace insists on in the *Ars Poetica*:

> *denique sit quodvis, simplex dumtaxat et unum* (23).
>
> So then, let your work be what you like, but at least let it be simple and unified.

Horace begins the ode in sight of a wintry landscape, and ends it with the command to make love now, while green springtime is at hand. But we are only apt to think the poem ill thought out or disjointed if we limit the words in *iunctura* to their dictionary meanings. It may be questionable etymology to pass from *virens* and *vir* and *viridis* to *ver,* but there is in the combination *virenti canities* (the green bloom of youth / the white hair of old age) a clear suggestion of spring / winter—enough to indicate that the poem need not be taken as a monologue spoken against realistic backdrops (though the backdrops are there and winter's at least is fully detailed). The poem seems rather a meditation in which, as so often in Horace, the landscapes are intended to mirror the seasons of man's life. The ratio

virenti	*canities*
youth	old age
green	white
spring	winter

reminds us that, in the poem, Thaliarchus is a *puer* while the Horace of the Odes is approaching middle age; that the warring winds of the third stanza may stand for passionate youth which gives way, when the gods so ordain, to old age (*veteres . . . orni*) and death (*cupressi*); that the opening stanza (the mountain covered with snow, the trees bent under their burden, the rivers halted by the ice) is as much a description of *canities* in all its associations as the closing stanzas (playing fields, whispers, and lovemaking) are of *virenti*.[27]

Each of the two words has a specific meaning, but within the structure of the poem it refuses to so limit itself; casting influence "to right and left and over the whole" it points to larger possibilities of interpretation. The associations the two words carry are what gives the poem its meaning.

If we think of the Odes of Horace as simple prose statements—if like some interlinear translator, we mentally rearrange the component words in prose order—we are likely to find ourselves saying, with Tyrrell, that Horace "did not much trouble himself whether the train of ideas was consecutive, or indeed whether there was any regular march of thought at all."[28] Worse, we may join the insensitive objectors who dismiss Horace because he forever mouths the same Epicurean platitudes and never says anything original or important. Such judgments are based on the false assumption that the meaning of a poem can be reduced to a prose summary, a paraphrase. Poetry is not made to communicate such meanings. In an ode of Horace every word plays a part. Any poet worth his salt will tell you that is the way it must be.

"Why do you want to write poetry?" W. H. Auden asks a hopeful beginner. "If the young man answers: 'I have important things to say,' then he is not a poet. If he answers: 'I like hanging around words listening to what they say,' then maybe he is going to be a poet."[29]

3

SOUNDS

"The sound must seem an Echo to the sense."—POPE

AT THE VERY TIME Horace was at work on the Odes, the rhetorician Dionysius of Halicarnassus was teaching in Rome that each letter has a special effect on the listener: among the vowels, long *a,e,o,u,i,* in that order, please the ear, while the short vowels, especially *e,* are unpleasant; *l,* easily the most agreeable of the semi-vowels, is soothing; *r,* the noblest, stirs to action; *m* and *n* imitate the sound of musical instruments; *s* is unpleasant, very much so if used repeatedly.[1] Dionysius was speaking about Greek, but his remarks would not be meaningless to a Latin poet working in Aeolian meters. Romans too were interested in sound. A Roman poet's works were intended, from the start, for recitation, and his public was accustomed to hearing finished oratorical periods in public and reading aloud in private. Cicero advises orators to search out fair-sounding words—even if thereby the grammar suffers; he also remarks that poets pay more attention to sound than to sense:

vocibus magis quam rebus inserviunt.[2]

If Cicero, in this casual aside, is speaking of apprentices in the art, many poets will agree. Witness Ezra Pound: "Let the candidate fill his mind with the finest cadences he can discover, preferably in a foreign language, so that the meaning of the words may be less likely to divert his attention from the movement," and again, "Let the neophyte know assonance and alliteration, rhyme immediate and delayed, simple and polyphonic, as a musician would expect to know harmony and counterpoint and all the minutiae of his craft."[3]

The Odes of Horace have nothing like the fine cadences of Virgil's *Aeneid*, or those poems unsurpassed for sheer beauty of sound, the *Georgics*. Horace's precise Aeolic stanza-forms admit no metrical variation, and as a result he must be content with musical effects of a more modest nature—the effects made by different-sounding words within the uniform patterns.

Let us not consider the meters for the moment, but concentrate first on the sound of the letters and words themselves.

Alliteration and Assonance

Older Latin writers, Ennius in particular, were to our taste excessive in their use of alliteration. Horace reserves the device for special effects, e.g., in a poem in praise of pristine virtue, he speaks in Ennian terms in the first line:

a*ngustam* a*mice* p*au*p*eriem* p*ati* (3.2.1)

and the last:

deseruit p*ede* P*oena claudo.*

The ode's most famous stanza rather overdoes it:

d*ulce et* d*ecorum est* p*ro* p*atria* m*ori:*
m*ors et fugacem* p*ersequitur virum,*
nec p*arcit imbellis iuventae*
p*o*p*litibus* t*imidove* t*ergo* (13-16).

The excess here may be intentional. Most of the alliteration in the Odes is neatly and subtly patterned:

celeris s*picula* C*ynthiae, / summo carmine*
(3.28.12-13);

> *Siculum* m*are* / *Poeno* p*urpureum* *sanguine* mol*libus* (2.12.2-3),

or combined with assonance:

> *non dec*o*lo*r*av*e*r*e *caedes*
> *quae caret* ore *c*r*uo*re *nostro* (2.1.35-36),

and humor:

> *magna*s in*ter* *ope*s ino*p*s (3.16.28).

The interplay of *m, t,* and *a* in the following is carefully composed:

> Ma*rt*em *tunic*a *t*ec*tum* a*d*ama*nti*n*a* (1.6.13).

Here the thumping of *t* against *em* fades into liquid *l*:

> Tem*pe* *to*t*id*em to*ll*i*t*e l*audibus* (1.21.9).

Assonance, perhaps originally used in maxims as a memory aid, crops up in Horace's more sententious or eulogistic moments:

> *om*ne ne*fas* *ani*mo mo*ventes* (3.4.68)
>
> *nobi*le le*tum* (1.12.36)
>
> *gran*de de*cus* (2.17.4).

That Horace regards these as pardonable lapses may be inferred from a passage in the *Ars Poetica*:

> *sunt delic*ta ta*men* *quibus ignovisse velimus* (347).
>
> there are some slips we may choose to overlook.

Again, most instances of assonance in the Odes are carefully patterned:

> *sp*erne *pu*er ne*que* (1.9.16)
>
> *q*uem *tu* Mel*pomene* *s*emel (4.3.1);

especially in the line which Wilkinson calls "an almost perfect chiasmus of sound":[4]

*qu*alem minis*trum* *ful*minis al*it*em (4.4.1),

and in:

p*au*per*i* re*cluditu*r / reg*umque* puer*is* (2.18.33-34)

—this last from a poem which specializes in the carefully placed anagram:

tamen . . . manet (29, 31),

and in repetition:

truditur dies die (15)

Tantalum atque Tantali (37)

vocatus atque non vocatus (40).

Repetition

There is a good deal of this verbal repetition in the Odes. In many cases it adds solemnity to the passage and at the same time eliminates the need for a weak connective:

terruit urbem, / terruit gentes (1.2.4-5)

audiet cives acuisse ferrum
quo graves Persae melius perirent,
audiet pugnas (21-23).[5]

But often the repetition serves no syntactical purpose. It is romantic:

dulce ridentem Lalagen amabo,
dulce loquentem (1.22.23-24),

or sorrowful:

eheu fugaces Postume, Postume (2.14.1),

or resolute:

ibimus, ibimus (2.17.10),

or triumphant:

audivere, Lyce, di *mea vota,* di
audivere, Lyce (4.13.1-2).[6]

or mocking:

et refugit te, *quia luridi*
dentes te, *quia rugae*
turpant et *capitis nives* (4.13.10-12),

Perhaps most noteworthy is Horace's use of short, repeated pronouns as connectives:

te *greges centum Siculaeque circum*
mugiunt vaccae, tibi *tollit hinnitum*
apta quadrigis equa, te *bis Afro*
muricae tinctae (2.16.33-36),

especially in the serious or humorous treatment of Roman prayer formulae, addressing Mercury (1.10:*te . . . te . . . te . . . tu*), Bacchus (2.19:*tu . . . tu . . . tu . . . te*), or a pious wine jar (3.21:*tu . . . tu . . . tu . . . te*).[7]

Individual letters

As Dionysius of Halicarnassus noted, the repetition of the letter *s* can be most unpleasant. Horace used the sound effectively in three derisory lines in which the letter, in combination with *i*, is almost hissed into the ear of an aging courtesan:

fis anus, et tamen
vis formosa videri
ludisque et bibis impudens. (4.13.2-4).

Horace also uses *s* in combination, first with *i*, then with *a*, to describe the whistling of the wind in the portentous storms that followed the murder of Caesar:

iam satis terris nivis atque dirae
grandinis misit Pater et rubente
dextera sacras iaculatus arces
terruit urbem (1.2.1-4),

and the hiss of Cleopatra's asp:

fortis et asperas / tractare serpentes (1.37.26-27).

If, as Robert Graves thinks, "the art of poetry consists in knowing exactly how to manipulate the letter *s*,"[8] then Horace showed his mastery of the art when he described, in ugly words and sounds, the dropsy:

crescit indulgens sibi dirus hydrops,
nec sitim pellit, nisi causa morbi
fugerit venis et aquosus albo
corpore languor (2.2.13-16).

The hard sound of the Latin *c*, especially in combination with liquid *r*, adds an extra dimension of tough malevolence to Horace's taunt that blazing lust will rage around Lydia's ulcerous liver:

circa iecur ulcerosum (1.25.15),

whereas *r* in combination with less harsh consonants can suggest the rising of the wind-storm:

motus orientis Austri et
aequoris nigri fremitum et trementes
verbere ripas (3.27.22-24).

And the contrast between the long and short quantities of the letter *o* has probably never been used so expressively as in the falling cadence at the end of 4.7:

vincula Pirithoo.

Elision

Horace does not resort to elision as often as Catullus and earlier writers, but there are instances in the Odes of elision being used, à la Catullus,[9] purposely and by way of illustration. God humbles the mighty:

insign(em) attenuat (1.34.13),

Hercules in his labors smashes through Hades:

perrupit Acheront(a) Herculeus labor (1.3.36),[10]

and shade trees intertwine their branches:

umbr(am) hospitalem consociar(e) amant (2.3.10).

The most emphatic use of elision occurs between lines. The three elisions at the end of 2.3, one of them hypermetrical, hurry the reader on relentlessly to Charon's skiff:

sors exitur(a) et nos in aetern(um)
exili(um) impositura cumbae.

Hypermeter marks the faltering speech of a lover:

cur facunda parum decor(o)
inter verba cadit lingua silentio? (4.1.35-36),

the whinny of a horse (reinforced by *i*- and *t*-sounds):

tibi tollit hinnit(um)
apta quadrigis equa (2.16.34-35),

and the very meaning of the verb *eximit*:

Phraaten
dissidens plebi numero beator(um)
eximit Virtus (2.2.17-19).

Rhyme

Rhyme is a feature so natural to Latin, particularly when a noun and its adjective are separated in the long hexameter line, that Roman poets hardly strive consciously to obtain rhymed effects. The first lines we read in the Odes would probably satisfy Pound's expectation of "rhyme immediate and delayed, simple and polyphonic." Eight of the first twelve verses may be said to have internal rhyme, and the remaining four rhyme at the end with others in the section:

*Maecenas atav*is *edite regib*us,
*o et praesidium et dulce decus me*um,

> *sunt quos curriculo pulverem Olympic*um
> *collegisse iuvat, metaque fervid*is
> *evitata rot*is *palmaque nobil*is
> *terrarum domin*os *evehit ad de*os;
> *hunc, si mobil*ium *turba Quirit*ium
> *certat tergemin*is *tollere honorib*us;
> *illum, si propri*o *condidit horre*o
> *quidquid de Libyc*is *verritur are*is.
> *gaudentem patrios findere sarcul*o
> *agros Attalic*is *condicionib*us
> *nunquam dimove*as . . . (1.1.1-13)

But one wonders whether Horace actually calculated this. The effect comes naturally enough, and if, as Gilbert Murray observes, "the purpose of rhyme is to mark clearly the end of the line and to provide the ear with a fixed resting place,"[11] then Horace can largely dispense with it because his meters themselves are so clearly structured.

Before we pass on to consider those meters, an *apologia* is perhaps in order. Much that follows is a matter of subjective, personal response and is likely to irritate those who are less than convinced that poets, and Latin poets in particular, hold to Pope's dictum "the sound must seem an echo to the sense." Horace seldom resorted to what we should call onomatopoeia, at least in its crudest form. His words and rhythms do not often imitate sounds; rather they express, time and again, the emotional content of the poems. The words applied by Dionysius of Halicarnassus to Homer will do as well for Horace:

> The most accomplished writers of both poetry and prose will even . . . with the most devoted artistry, fit their syllables to the very emotions they want to represent
>
> (*De Structura Orationis* 15).

Horace himself urges the poet to be sensitive to sounds, to send ill-shaped verses back to the anvil, striking out lines that are sluggish (*inertes*), flat (*duros*) and unrhythmical (*incomptis*).[12] But he is no advocate of mere euphony: some liberties must be taken, otherwise, he says, a man's poetry will be only beyond reproach, when it might have been beyond praise:

> *vitavi denique culpam,*
> *non laudem merui* (*AP* 267-68).

And when he states that certain meters are appropriate only to certain literary genres it is largely on the basis of "the very emotions they want to represent"—hexameter for *tristia bella,* elegaic couplet for *querimonia,* iambics for *rabies,* lyric meters for *iuvenum curas et libera vina.*[13]

Expressive language need not be directly imitative. There is no mention of grunts or thumps or thuds

> when Ajax strives some rock's vast weight to throw,

nor swish or whir or whistle

> when swift Camilla scours the plain,
> Flies o'er th' unbending corn, and skims along the main.[14]

Horace is no less accomplished than his eighteenth-century disciple. He asks only that his reader keep his ears open. What we must listen for is the sound of the word in combination with the step of the meter. "The meter is an ideal pattern which is . . . uniform throughout the whole poem. (But) no single verse or stanza, as spoken, is exactly identical in rhythm with any other. In every verse the words conform to the meter with more or less variation."[15] It is to that variation that we must listen.

In considering the sound of Horace's meters, the all-but-defeating factor is the fundamental difference between Greek and Latin poetry, which is quantitative, and modern English poetry, which is accentual. In the following considerations I shall ask the reader to make the effort, as best he can and in what way he can, to prolong the long syllables and lighten the short ones. The easiest method is to resort to stress, placing at least a slight accent on each long syllable. Obviously this is a far from satisfactory expedient. But Gilbert Murray observes, "I cannot help believing that what the ancients called 'length,' and what we call 'stress,' and what some Far Eastern nations, I believe, call 'tone,' are psychologically all subdivisions of 'importance,' or 'the quality attended to.' "[16] It seems fairly certain that Latin verse, at an early stage of its development, was accentual (witness the importance of accent in scanning Plautus); certainly it fell neatly into accentual rhythms in the Middle Ages. If the accent did not entirely disappear when Latin was wedded to Greek meters, then we may believe that, as T. S. Eliot puts it, "part of the pleasure in the poetry arose from the presence in it of two metrical schemes in a kind of counterpoint."[17] The normal rhythm of human speech either clashed or coincided with the rhythm of the meter.

Sapphics

The Sapphic stanza is best suited to illustrating the difficulty. Sapphics composed in the Middle Ages,[18] and countless *alma mater* songs since then, have fixed the rhythm of the long line in the stanza as

Ínteger vítae scélerísque púrus.

The metrical accents here are coincident with normal speech rhythms. Horace's line, however, is

Íntegér vítaé scelerísque púrus.

There are two clashes here (the metrical accents on the syllables *-ger* and *-tae*), and the line is a good deal slower than the rhythm we are accustomed to in later musical settings.

Actually Horace himself is responsible for the difficulty with the Sapphic stanza. In adapting Sappho's original line:

— ∪ — $\underline{\cup}$ — ∪∪ — ∪ — $\underline{\cup}$

he regularly lengthened the fourth syllable and placed a marked caesura after the fifth:

— ∪ — — — || ∪∪ — ∪ — ⏓

Sappho's rippling trochaic line was slowed, at half point, to a halt. And if a word ends at the fifth syllable, normal Latin speech rhythms (accenting the penult) would lighten the fifth and stress the fourth syllable—so much so that Horace himself had to instruct the chorus who sang his Sapphic *Carmen Saeculare,*

Lesbium servate pedem (4.6.35)

Keep to Sappho's meter.[19]

Suffice it to say, in a discussion I hope to keep as non-technical as possible, that in Horace's hands the Sapphic stanza is weighted, made stately and solemn. We have noted before that Sapphics are appropriate for reasoned, lapidary statements. The three metrically identical long lines are in fact so connected that Horace reserves his special effects, musical, humorous, or epigrammatic, for the trailing short line, the adonic:

— ∪∪ — ⏓

It is here that our attention is directed, whether the brief phrase be a three-step, all but onomatopoeic:

ter pede terram (3.18.16),

or a surprise:

risit Apollo (1.10.12),

or a word to the wise:

linque severa (3.8.28),

or a signature:

vatis Horati (4.6.44).

Bellerophon fills the adonic with his weight and bulk when Pegasus shakes him off:

terret ambustus Phaëthon avaras
spes, et exemplum grave praebet ales
Pegasus terrenum equitem gravatus
Bellerophontem (4.11.25-28),

as does Mercury, when he trails the other gods:

fervidus tecum puer et solutis
Gratiae zonis properentque Nymphae
et parum comis sine te Iuventas
Mercuriusque (1.30.5-8).

It is a pleasant experience, after reading a poem in Sapphics, to re-read it in brief (seeing the movie in a series of stills) by casting the eye back over the adonics. A long, complex poem such as 1.2, serious in its political implications, almost comic in its mythological asides, is summed up by a mere listing of the brief musical phrases which complete its stanzas:

terruit urbem
Rome is in terror

visere montes
flooding the mountains

aequore dammae
deer in the water

templaque Vestae
temples demolished

-xorius amnis
Tiber o'erflowing[20]

rara iuventus
thinned ranks of offspring

carmina Vestam
what prayer will save us?

augur Apollo
tell us, Apollo

respicis auctor
Mars, look upon us

vultus in hostem
enemy warfare

Caesaris ultor
vengeance for Caesar

ocior aura
swept off too quickly

te duce, Caesar
Caesar our leader.

Wilkinson is certainly right in feeling that the Sapphic is less than satisfactory for longer poems: "No amount of enjambment can prevent the adonic from reining us in as often as we get going."[21] It might be said, however, that the longer the poem (e.g., 3.11 or 3.27) the more vivid and vigorous the adonic. And that even the weighty, concentrated long lines can be made to serve a purpose in a long poem: in paying tribute to meter-less free-wheeling Pindar (*immensus, numerisque . . . lege solutis* 4.2.7, 11-12), Horace not only uses hypermetrical lines, but also casts his statement in the most rigid of his meters and then violates his own rule for the caesura twelve times![22]

Asclepiads

The Asclepiad meters are best approached via the choriamb (— ◡◡ —). To this basic foot, a spondee is prefixed and an iamb or single syllable appended, to form the various Asclepiad lines,
pherecratean:

— — — ◡◡ — ⏓

glyconic:

— — — ◡◡ — ◡⏓

lesser Asclepiad:

— — —⏑⏑— || —⏑⏑— ⏑⏓

greater Asclepiad:

— — —⏑⏑— || —⏑⏑— || —⏑⏑— ⏑⏓

Five separate metrical schemes are formed by using these four varieties singly or in combination. The resulting meters are lighter than the long Sapphic line—indeed, with Asclepiads, the longer the line, the lighter the effect. The regular caesurae are another of our poet's innovations, and as Latin is fairly well stocked with choriambic words, Horace is able, if he chooses, to fill every foot with a word or phrase of its own:

portum | *nonne vides* | *ut* (1.14.3)
lymphae | *desiliunt* | *tuae* (3.13.16)
nigro | *compulerit* | *Mercurius* | *gregi* (1.24.18)
quae nunc | *oppositis* | *debilitat* | *pumicibus* | *mare* (1.11.5).

Such effects are not always desirable. But the gentle lilt[23] of the self-contained choriambic word may well have prompted the choice of Asclepiad meters for odes dealing with Virgilius, Quintilius, Mercurius, Melpomene, Asterie, Leuconoë, and the Fons Bandusiae, and suggested such phrases as *o quid agis* (1.14.2), *sparge rosas* (3.19.22), *parce, precor* (4.1.2), and *carpe diem* (1.11.8).

Alcaics

In adapting Alcaeus' stanza to his own purposes, Horace almost invariably observed the caesura after the fifth syllable in the first two lines, and regularly lengthened the fifth syllable there and in the third line as well. Alcaeus' quick trochaic movement was thus calmed and halted. The result is a marvelous combination of strength and delicacy:

⏓ —⏑ — — || —⏑⏑ —⏑ ⏓
⏓ —⏑ — — || —⏑⏑ —⏑ ⏓

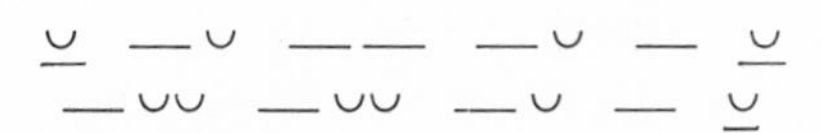

Gilbert Murray's enthusiastic description of Alcaeus' stanza is still the best: "There is symmetry between 1 and 2, symmetry between 3 and 4; but 4 is the perfect rhythm, smooth and untroubled, at which 3 is an approximation or 'attempt,' and to which all three verses lead by a kind of progress. The last verse of an alcaic is extraordinarily delightful in rhythm; but it would be nothing in particular if it were not reached by a struggle—and just the right kind of struggle."[24] It might be said further that Horace's restructured long lines are each composed of statement, pause, and release. The third line then repeats and echoes the first half of the long lines: it is statement, labored and slow (more often than not it will contain only two short syllables), a solemn, unsuccessful attempt at metrical solution. The fourth line is then an echo of the second half of the long lines: dactylic and light, a completely satisfying release.[25]

In the face of this achievement, Wilkinson allows himself to exclaim, "Horace's Alcaic stanza is a triumph." He regards the third line, and in particular the lengthened fifth syllable in the middle of the third line, as "the pivot of the stanza."[26] And indeed the laborious struggle in that line, working toward the release it finds in the fourth, is used scores of times by Horace as an echo of sound to sense:

> *té rúrsus in béllúm resórbéns*
> *únda fretís tulit áestuósís* (2.7.15-16)

> a wave, sucking you back into the fray,
> bore you off amid seething billows.

It is as if the wave that threatened Pompeius slowly crested and then suddenly carried him off in a burst of foam. Similar reversals of motion in both sound and sense abound:

> *pronos relabi posse rivos*
> *montibus et Tiberim reverti* (1.29.11-12)

descending streams can glide backwards
on the mountains, and the Tiber change
its course;

nec saevus ignis nec tremendo
Iuppiter ipse ruens tumultu (1.16.11-12)

nor savage fire, nor Jupiter himself,
crashing down in shuddery shock;

vexare turmas et frementem
mittere equum medios per ignes (4.14.23-24)

to overthrow the enemy troops and
drive his snorting charger through the midst
of the flames;

consultus erro, nunc retrorsum
vela dare atque iterare cursus (1.34.3-4)

smugly going astray, now I must
tack my sails about and retrace my course.[27]

The river in 3.29 sometimes glides slowly and hypermetrically into the sea, sometimes sweeps before it stones and rubble, cattle and homes in a restless movement that overflows the stanza:

cum pace delabentis Etrusc(um)
in mare, nunc lapides adesos

stirpesque raptas et pecus et domos
volventis una . . . (35-38).

There are many examples of rest giving way to motion:

non rura quae Liris quieta
mordet aqua taciturnus amnis (1.31.7-8)

nor the meadows whose margin, with placid
flow, the Liris eats away, a silent stream;

ad arma cessantes ad arma
concitet imperiumque frangat (1.35.15-16)

"to arms, to arms" the wavering ones
it may arouse, and smash the ruling power;

vivaeque producent lucernae,
dum rediens fugat astra Phoebus (3.21.23-24)

and burning torches will attend you
till Phoebus returning routs the stars.

One ode to Venus builds steadily through its three stanzas toward the release in the last line:

regina, sublimi flagello
tange Chloën semel arrogantem (3.26.11-12)

o queen, raise your lash on high and
strike arrogant Chloë, just once.

Perhaps the finest examples of heavy spondaic third and moving dactylic fourth line are found in the finished Alcaic stanzas of the six Roman odes in Book III:

coetusque vulgares et udam
spernit humum fugiente penna (3.2.23-24)

the common throng and the dank earth
it spurns in its winged flight;

errare per lucos, amoenae
quos et aquae subeunt et aurae (3.4.7-8)

to wander through groves
that lovely waters and breezes haunt;

Titanas immanemque turbam
fulmine sustulerit caduco (3.4.43-44)

a great swarm of Titans
he uprooted with hurtling thunderbolt;

interque maerentes amicos
egregius properaret exsul (3.5.47-48)

among his sorrowing friends
he hastened forth, a glorious exile;

hoc fonte derivata clades
in patriam populumque fluxit (3.6.19-20)

channeled from this source, disaster
has flowed forth on country and people;

bobus fatigatis, amicum
tempus agens abeunte curru (3.6.43-44)

(lifting the yoke) from the weary oxen,
bringing on night as his chariot departs.

A poet reveals himself most when he takes subtle liberties with his own scheme. The structure of the fourth Alcaic line is almost recast in 3.1.16, as the dactylic rhythm is frustrated by five two-syllable words. The reader can only with difficulty muster:

ómne capáx movet úrna nómen.

The impact of the words on the printed page[28] and the force of the speech accent almost force one to read the line:

ómne cápax móvet úrna nómen.

There are no light-hearted dactyls here; the tossing of lots in the urn of fate is a measured, irrevocable movement.

This line perhaps more than any other cited illustrates how Horace's sound is expressive without being unduly literal. His words quicken his meters. If I may quote Gilbert Murray one last time, "words are material objects and therefore more or less recalcitrant. They seek to obey the (metrical) law, but having an independent life of their own, they obey it always with a difference."[29] They coincide or clash, expanding or contracting the contour of the metrical line, which is quickened (remembering Aristotle's "live animal" we had better say animated) by the sound of the words within it.

4

IMAGES

"The greatest thing by far is to be a master of metaphor, and this is the one thing that cannot be learned from others."

—Aristotle

Poetry never explains. It simply presents us with rhythmed words. Yet when we have examined the words and sounds in a poem we have not reached its inner life, or touched on the process in the poet that produced the poem. There is still the image.

Poets are image-makers. They speak, not with the conventional logic of the prose-writer, but with the special logic of the imagination. They present us, not with carefully reasoned statements, but with images in verse. Ezra Pound defines the image as "that which presents an intellectual and emotional complex in an instant of time."[1] He is speaking, of course, as an "imagist" of the early years of this century. Horace's approach is something else again. But his images are not unlike Pound's: they carry both intelligible meaning and emotional overtones. To Pound's workable definition I should like only to add that under the term "image" I mean to include not only simile and metaphor but any picture, indeed any sensory suggestion.

Though there is no lack of literary histories and handbooks which describe him as deficient in imagination, Horace can call up an image as beautifully as any poet, and with more economy than most:

fidens iuventus horrida bracchiis (3.4.50)

a proud band of stalwarts, bristling with arms;

sol ubi montium / mutaret umbras (3.6.41-42)

when the sun shifted the shadows on the mountains;

condit quisque diem collibus in suis (4.5.29)

each man puts the day away in his own hills.

He can also strew details about with a "frightful realism"[2] which has offended Romantic poets and Victorian critics:

quia luridi
dentes te, quia rugae
turpant et capitis nives (4.13.10-12).

because yellow teeth and wrinkles make you ugly, and snow on your head.

Thracio bacchante magis sub inter-
lunia vento,

cum tibi flagrans amor et libido,
quae solet matres furiare equorum,
saeviet circa iecur ulcerosum (1.25.11-15).

as the Thracian wind rises to a shriek
on those moonless nights, when blazing
passion and lust—such as drives mares mad
in the pack—shall rage about your ulcerous
liver.

These pictures, be they fanciful or Romantic or repulsive, are not mere ornament. Horace is the very critic who condemns the "purple patch," who begins his *Ars Poetica* by insisting that a work of art must be consistent in its pictures, must pattern its imagery.[3] He is virtually alone among ancient literary critics in sounding this note. While Aristotle, Cicero, Longinus, Quintilian, and their lesser colleagues treat figures of speech from many different points of view, they invariably regard them as so much ornament, mere literary devices or aids to rhetoric. With Horace, they are integral. His images cannot be excised from the poem without the structure collapsing. Take as an example the famous epilogue to the first three books of the Odes:

Exegi monumentum aere perennius
regalique situ pyramidum altius,
quod non imber edax, non Aquilo impotens
possit diruere aut innumerabilis
annorum series et fuga temporum.
non omnis moriar, multaque pars mei
vitabit Libitinam: usque ego postera
crescam laude recens, dum Capitolium
scandet cum tacita virgine pontifex.
dicar, qua violens obstrepit Aufidus
et qua pauper aquae Daunus agrestium
regnavit populorum, ex humili potens
princeps Aeolium carmen ad Italos
deduxisse modos. sume superbiam
quaesitam meritis et mihi Delphica
lauro cinge volens, Melpomene, comam (3.30).

I have completed a monument more lasting than
  bronze,
And more exalted than the mouldering grandeur of the pyramids,
One which no destructive rain or blustering
  windstorm
Can topple, nor the passage of time immemorial,
Nor the flight of the ages.
I shall not altogether die, no—a great part of me
Will escape the death-Venus. I shall live on and
  on,
Ever new with the praise of posterity, so long as
The high priest mounts the Capitol with the
  silent virgin.

I shall be sung, where the wild Aufidus roars
And where Daunus, poor in water, ruled
Over country folk—I, risen to power from low degree,
The first to have wed Greek song to Latin meters.
Accept the pride-of-place I have won
For you, Melpomene, and graciously
Crown my hair with Delphic laurel.

If we attempt to "get past the poetic language," to determine "just what Horace is saying" by clipping away the images, the entire first sentence (metaphor likening Horace's achievement to a monument) must go. So must *multaque pars mei / vitabit Libitinam* (mythological). So must *dum Capitolium / scandet cum tacita virgine pontifex* and *qua pauper aquae Daunus agrestium / regnavit populorum* (topical references). And the entire last sentence (mythological). We are left with:

non omnis moriar
usque ego postera / crescam laude recens
dicar
ex humili potens
princeps Aeolium carmen ad Italos / deduxisse modos.

A not unsatisfactory précis of the poem—yet we note on closer inspection that the first four phrases form a single image (the survival of man's immortal part, magnified, hymned, and risen from its mortal estate), and that this complements the pattern of images already excised (the weather-beaten grave marker, the flight of time, the death-goddess, religious ritual and Horace's birthplace). And the last of the phrases, Horace's proud claim to have been the first to write Latin lyric poetry in the Greek style, is certainly a metaphor of some sort, though the problem of interpreting *deduxisse* (a marriage? the weaving of warp and woof? the founding of a new colony?) is almost as difficult as explaining *Aeolium carmen* and *Italos modos.*

The entire poem is cast in images. But the figurative language does not call attention to itself. Most of it does not even evoke precise sensory impressions. The famous phrases in 3.30 are neither similes nor metaphors nor mythological allusions. They are vigorous statements which distill the associations of the images surrounding them.

A further point. 3.30 would not be any clearer a statement if Horace had appended an explanation of his imagery. It would in fact be reduced to something less than a poem. Horace trusts his images to make their own effect. And in so doing he is appealing to the very sources of poetry in his audience—to the associations, memories, wishes, and dreams each one of us has collected. Part of the appeal of poetry is (if I may be permitted a brief Jungian aside) to our personal share in what psychologists call, variously, "myth" or "the group dream" or "the archetype." The great symbols of existence are as much in evidence in Horace's Odes as they are in Mallarmé. Wind and water, fire and flowers, wine and gods recur in almost predictable patterns, not because Horace always intends it so, but simply because he thinks imaginatively. These images are seldom, if ever, symbols with separate meanings. The reader is not tempted to attach a fixed significance to them as he finds them again and again in the poems. But he does respond, partly because of personal associations, partly because he recalls other passages in the poems where the same images come together in similar combinations. As one grows more familiar with the Odes, one discovers that Horace's images are, consciously or no, patterned just as his words and sounds are. His appeal goes past the mind, the eye, and the ear to the imaginative region beyond these.

"There is a kind of image that is natural to one poet and not to another," says John Ciardi as he lists the images most commonly found in the poetry of Donne:

knots
anchors

royal crowns
the king's face
coins
the king's image on a coin
candles in darkness

"all of them . . . images that concentrate power in a small space." He concludes that "a simple tabulation of the kind of image that appears in a man's poetry is one index to his mind."[4] One thinks of Jean Cocteau, exploring problems of self-identity in terms of gloves and masks, mirrors and doors and infernal machines. It is not improper, I hope, to mention in this connection the parables of Christ, with their direct and homely images:

wheat and cockle
a grain of mustard seed
leaven
a treasure hidden in a field
a single pearl of great price
a net full of fish of every kind.

That these are used for a didactic purpose does not detract from their value as poetic images—evoking response, creating in simple folk a close sense of identification with "the kingdom of heaven." They speak eloquently of the image-making mind of their Author.

What sort of images does Horace use? Many of his figures are mythological and, unfortunately, the associations they stir in present-day readers are all too conventional. Horace's Muses, for example, do little to fire the twentieth-century imagination. Though they may dress occasionally as Roman Camenae, we are not fooled; they are the standard Greek figures, and no amount of talk about their mountains, grottoes, and springs can make them really come alive. The Olympians, each of them capable of playing a score of mythological roles, seem almost typecast in traditional parts. The rivers, gods, and denizens of the underworld are stock reminders of death. Must we dismiss Horace, then, as a trivial dealer in plaster figurines?

It cannot be said that these and other figures of myth and legend have in the Odes anything like the power they wield in the Homeric poems or in Greek drama. Yet Horace's gentle gods awaken in him a variety of response ranging from religious awe to tongue-in-cheek. This is so because he sees his mythological figures not as symbols with fixed meanings, but as images—bright pictures touched with personal associations. The problem lies, not with Horace's lack of imagination, but with the modern reader's conditioning. He must think and feel his way past the slag heaps accumulated by those centuries which specialized in the abuse of the mythological allusion. The tendency to regard all mythology as so much literary clap-trap can be overcome only by a serious mental effort to dissociate Venus and the Graces, Bacchus and Phoebus and the rest from the maze of callous and frigid references to them in late Renaissance and neo-classic poetasters. The real gods and heroes of Greece can be rediscovered in our own consciousness. It is imperative that we search them out if we are to respond to any degree to some of Horace's most evocative stanzas:

te Liber et, si laeta aderit, Venus
segnesque nodum solvere Gratiae
vivaeque producent lucernae,
dum rediens fugat astra Phoebus
(3.21.21-24),

Bacchus and Venus (if she come with gladness)
and the Graces, disinclined to break their bond,
and burning torches—all these will escort you,
till Phoebus returning routs the stars,

or if we are to believe him at all when he solemnly asserts:

me nec Chimaerae spiritus igneae
nec, si resurgat, centimanus Gyas

divellet umquam: sic potenti
Iustitiae placitumque Parcis
(2.17.13-16).

the fire-breathing Chimera will not tear me from you, nor hundred-handed Gyas, should he rise against me. Mighty Justice and the Fates have willed it so.

A list of the non-mythological images most commonly used by Horace would certainly include:

snow
storms at sea
purple garments
the rich man who extends his domain out over the water
the heir who waits with greedy hands to inherit the earth.

Are these an index to the mind of Horace? We might note that all of these carry sinister connotations for him. Snow (and ice and winter and white) are nature's death;[5] storms at sea bring us face to face with destruction;[6] purple is an excess to be avoided, a reminder of how fragile is the mortal it bedecks;[7] the rich man who makes land on the sea is more than excessive—his rage to live is unnatural.[8] All are reminders of death, but the most forbidding of these images is the heir, a gloomy figure from the Satires[9] who makes his appearance in Horace's most beautiful odes[10] to remind us that the coming generation will have little respect for the goods we store away.

None of these images is a *symbol* of death. But all carry somber associations. As with words, so it is possible to speak of images in terms of denotation and connotation. They denote certain pictures or sense experiences, and connote emotional overtones. In recent years, the French symbolist poets have been mined and cross-indexed. We have been given elaborate tabulations of the number of times a poet uses an image, the area of experience from which it is drawn, the associations it prompts, and so on. IBM computers are even put to this task. Obviously this sort of thing can get out of hand if too much importance is attached to it. But it yields certain dividends when applied to lyric art—and to Horace's Odes in particular.

We have listed some of the death-connoting images in the Odes. Horace's life-images tend to fall into two classes —liquid and vegetative. Though I have never seen an index to Horatian metaphor, I should hazard a guess that the images most often used in the Odes are of wine and flowers. Horace habitually thinks of our sweet but transient lives on earth as "days of wine and roses." Recently the wine-symbolism in Horace has been documented and interpreted: whether the wine is poured in libation (4.5.33), drunk in triumph (1.37.1), splashed by the heir on the pavement (2.14.26) or, as so often, used to dispel care and induce forgetfulness at the banquet, it invariably "represents a commitment to present life."[11] Roses too are life-images: they adorn the feast (2.3.14), the tête à tête (3.29.3), and the secluded grove (2.11.14) where the poet savors the sweetness of living. But they are melancholy images, impermanent, *nimium breves,* "ein Symbol der flüchtigen Lebensfreude."[12]

The two life-images are associated and all but inseparable. A mention of one will call forth the other:

non ante verso lene merum cado
cum flore, Maecenas, rosarum
(3.29.2-3).

gentle wine from a jug as yet un-
tipped,
and, Maecenas, the blossoms
of the rose.[13]

Occasionally the roses will be replaced by other blossoms:

verbenas, pueri, ponite turaque
bimi cum patera meri
(1.19.14-15).

my lads, put sprays of leaves and
incense here,
and a bowl of two-year-old wine.[14]

The response is so instinctive in Horace that he can extend this life-imagery to other liquid-vegetative pictures. Peaceful rivers and branches remind us to live and love while we may:

circa virentes est animus tuae
campos iuvencae, nunc fluviis gravem
solantis aestum, nunc in udo
ludere cum vitulis salicto
praegestientis

(2.5.5-9).

the thoughts of your beloved are (like a heifer's) turned towards green fields, as now she finds relief from the oppressive heat in the streams, and now delights to play with young calves among the wet willow trees.[15]

Conversely, water and trees tossed by storms mirror our struggles and sufferings:

cras foliis nemus
multis et alga litus inutili
demissa tempestas ab Euro
sternet

(3.17.9-12).

tomorrow a storm, unleashed from the East, will strew the grove with leaves and the shore with useless seaweed.[16]

In the Soracte ode, the opening stanza depicts winter's death as burdening the trees and freezing the rivers, while the second stanza, urging us to live in the present, is cast in terms of logs piled high on the hearth and wine freely flowing. I am not suggesting Horace consciously planned this. Only that, like all good poets, he thinks imaginatively, and that there is logic in the interrelation of his images. In 1.5 (*Quis multa gracilis*), the boy is *perfusus liquidis odoribus* in a somewhat desperate attempt to live life to the full *multa in rosa*, while the girl is not only unbedewed (*simplex munditiis*), she is fiery (Pyrrha), elementally opposed to water. Horace forecasts that the boy's liquid confidence will give way to disillusionment and finally disaster—expressed in terms of tears and a storm at sea; while he will nearly drown, she will doubtless remain high and dry (like the primeval Pyrrha who survived the flood), a siren in a seaside cave.[17]

There are meaningful life-images in *O Fons Bandusiae* as well. Commager persuasively argues that Horace intends this ode as "an invocation to his own art."[18] We may add then that in calling the spring

dulci digne mero non sine floribus
(3.13.2)

worthy of sweet wine, and flowers too

Horace implies that lyric art is worth devoting one's life to: the offering of life-images represents self-dedication. And, in an extension of the liquid-vegetative image, there is sacrificed the warm blood of a pubescent kid who gives promise of love and war: artistic creation demands that the artist forsake a career of pleasure and prestige. The closing stanza:

fies nobilium tu quoque fontium,
me dicente cavis impositam ilicem
saxis, unde loquaces
lymphae desiliunt tuae

thus implies that Horace's art will rank with the greatest of antiquity, as he sings of his experience in modest and characteristic terms—oak tree and leaping, babbling water. Doubtless Horace never intended the poem as a complete allegory, with the kid as symbol. There is only the pattern of his imagery to suggest more than the words denote.

Every ode[19] of Horace is more than the sum of its parts. Like Aristotle's "live animal," it is a living organism that is at once delicate and indestructible—words, sounds, and images in forcefully subtle relationships.

5

THOUGHT AND FEELING

"Evanescent visitations of thought and feeling . . . arising unforeseen and departing unbidden."

—SHELLEY

WHEN WORDS, SOUNDS, AND IMAGES conspire to a single purpose, the result is poetry:

quo pinus ingens albaque populus
umbram hospitalem consociare amant
ramis? quid obliquo laborat
lympha fugax trepidare rivo?

(2.3.9-12)

Why do the towering pine and white poplar love to make friendly shade together with their branches? Why does the rushing water struggle to hurry down the winding river-course?

"If the last seven words are not poetry," says T. E. Page, "it would be hard to say what is."[1] They most assuredly are poetry, and if it is hard to say why,[2] some of the observations we have made thus far may help us.

There is first an artful ordering of words. *pinus ingens albaque populus* suggests that the pine is dark as well as massy, and the poplar not only white but small; the "influence to right and left" effects a double antithesis. Further, the forest shade is allowed to color the last part of the stanza: both eye and ear respond to the effect of *ramis* overhanging, burdening line three. And there is much for the eye in those last seven words, which Horace has arranged into an extended chiasmus:

obliquo laborat / lympha fugax trepidare rivo

so that the winding stream contains the fleeting water as it struggles to press onward.

As for sounds, elisions mark the *Waldweben* of the second line:

umbr(am) hospitalem consociar(e) amant.

There is a deft solution of the Alcaic sound-sense problem: the heavy third line struggles, like the water in the stream, to the release of the fourth. And there is a notable sound effect in that fourth line. The end words in the line are joined to the center words by assonance:

*lym*pha fug*ax*[3] *trepida*re ri*vo,*

but the center of the line is marked by an almost onomatopoeic splash:

*fuga*x tr*epidare.*

The effect is emphasized by the clash of speech accent and metrical ictus at this point:

*lýmpha fugá*x tr*epidáre rívo.*

Finally, Horace has contrived to limit his use of the whispering letter *s* (and, with one exception, humming *m* and *n*) to the forest picture, while liquids *l* and *r* predominate in the description of the stream.

Felicitous as these effects are, they do not singly or together make poetry. The appeal to eye,[4] ear, and tongue serves mainly to awaken the imagination. "Why the lovely shade trees?" Horace wonders. "Why the rippling stream?" Such questions would not be asked by a Romantic poet. Wordsworth does not ask about the landscape; he is overwhelmed by it, as it speaks to his emotions and enlarges his soul. Such questions should not be asked by an Epicurean poet. Lucretius has answers instead. He sees through the landscape to the marvelous interaction of countless atoms beneath. But Horace, at his moments of deepest reflection, must ask these questions. Landscape is for him not some external object for his inspiration or inspection; it is nature's mirror of his own life. Horace's landscapes are inscapes: supple green springtime yielding to chill winter whiteness, fresh-blowing winds giving way to blustering storms at sea, and then stillness in the treetops. Water and trees, especially, hold the mirror up to man. And in this most beautiful of stanzas Horace makes them almost human:

consociare amant
laborat . . . trepidare.[5]

Horace's two questions apply as much to the cycle of human life as they do to nature's image of that cycle. They are imaginative language for "Why do we love?" "Why do we struggle?" "Has our life any meaning at all?"

The four lines are poetry, and great poetry, because they ask the most profound of questions in what is, for Horace, the most characteristically beautiful way.

It is often said of Horace that he lacked genuine feeling and had nothing important to say. This despite such statements as:

> *non satis est pulchra esse poemata; dulcia sunto,*
> *et quocumque volent animum auditoris agunto.*
> (*Ars Poetica* 99-100)

> it is not enough for poems to be pretty; let them be charming, *and* let them lead the listener's soul where they will.

The Odes have their depths of feeling and heights of illumination. It must only be borne in mind that Horace's insights and emotions are as carefully worked into his structures as are his words and rhythms, are as neatly patterned as his images. As the *Ars Poetica* and the other epistles on writing poetry clearly indicate, Horace did not think of art as the expression of a great idea or the communication of an overwhelming experience. We are not to look to him for the titanic achievements of Dante or Michelangelo, Beethoven or Dostoevski. He lived in times of great historic significance and was associated with important political figures, yet his thought remained simple and gently eclectic, his experience limited. He was at pains to keep it that way, preferring to dedicate himself completely to his art. If then we must look for great ideas or overwhelming experiences, they are not to be found *in* the poems. They *are* the poems. One hundred and three rhythmic Greek songs in Latin word-patterns, composed with a subtlety and imagination such as lyric poetry had not seen for five hundred years—these were Horace's great ideas and deep-felt experiences. Few of us can say we have had ideas so original, experiences so rich.

If the reader asks for genuine feeling and significant thought, let him read Horace's Odes with some attention to the structural interplay of word, sound, and image. Most of human living is there, and the important questions are asked.

PART II

Notes and Analyses

I

1.4: SONIC CIRCLE

Solvitur acris hiems grata vice veris et Favoni,
trahuntque siccas machinae carinas,
ac neque iam stabulis gaudet pecus aut arator igni,
nec prata canis albicant pruinis.

iam Cytherea choros ducit Venus imminente luna,
iunctaeque Nymphis Gratiae decentes
alterno terram quatiunt pede, dum graves Cyclopum
Vulcanus ardens urit officinas.

nunc decet aut viridi nitidum caput impedire myrto
aut flore terrae quem ferunt solutae;
nunc et in umbrosis Fauno decet immolare lucis,
seu poscat agna sive malit haedo.

pallida Mors aequo pulsat pede pauperum tabernas
regumque turres. o beate Sesti,
vitae summa brevis spem nos vetat incohare longam.
iam te premet nox fabulaeque Manes

et domus exilis Plutonia; quo simul mearis,
nec regna vini sortiere talis,
nec tenerum Lycidan mirabere, quo calet iuventus
nunc omnis et mox virgines tepebunt.

The bitter winter is breaking up, with the pleasant change to spring and the West Wind. Cranes are hauling thirsty ships to sea. Cattle no longer delight in their stalls, or ploughman at his fireside, and no longer are the meadows white with hoar frost.

Already Cytherean Venus leads the dance as the moon hangs low above, and the lovely Graces hand in hand with the nymphs beat the earth with answering step, while Vulcan, all ablaze, fires the mighty forges of the Cyclops.

Now is the fitting time to circle a shining head with green myrtle, or the blossoms which the freed earth bears. Now too is the time to sacrifice to Faunus in shadowy groves, if he demand an ewe lamb or prefer a male kid.

Ashen death knocks with an impartial foot at the hovels of the poor and the palaces of kings. O Sestius, happy though you be, life's brief span forbids us to cherish any long hopes. Soon night will close in on you, and the ghosts of myth,

and the prison-house of Pluto. Once you've entered there, you'll cast no more for mastery of the revels, and gaze no more on soft young Lycidas, for whom all the boys are now on fire, for whom the girls will soon begin to glow.

THE SPRING SONG to Sestius is a fine example of an ode fashioned almost wholly[1] from inter-related images. Every year, nature dramatizes the human life-cycle, but with an important difference: life and warmth return to the earth, but man sees no second spring. 1.4 is as much concerned with life and death as it is with spring and winter. But the ratio spring:winter::life:death is not immediately established. It is introduced by antithetic images—patterns of freedom:bondage, warmth:cold, green:white, light:darkness. The interplay of these is vigorous and unsubtle and may be briefly summarized.

In the first pattern, the triumph of spring over winter is imaginatively pictured as a release from bondage. The earth is freed from its seasonal enslavement (*solvitur*;

terrae . . . solutae); ships are hauled by chains down to sea; cattle leave their stalls and men their firesides. As winter means confinement, so in the end is death imprisoning (*premet nox . . . domus exilis Plutonia*). The triumph of spring can be expressed, then, in countercurrents—spring's freedom *in terms of* bondage (*iunctae . . . Gratiae*; *nunc decet . . . caput impedire myrto*).[2]

In the second pattern, spring's warmth is contrasted with winter's chill. *Acris hiems* gives way to the West Wind and Vulcan, all ablaze, fires the subterranean forges in anticipation, presumably, of Jupiter's spring thunderbolts. Even springtime lovemaking is presented in terms of heat (*calet iuventus*; *virgines tepebunt*). But again, there are countercurrents—winter's cold *in terms of* warmth (*stabulis gaudet pecus*; *arator igni*).

The third pattern, familiar enough from the Soracte ode,[3] interlays wintry white (*prata canis albicant pruinis*) and white hairs (*nitidum caput*)[4] and ashen death (*pallida Mors*) with springtime green (*viridi . . . myrto aut flore*) and tender youth (*tenerum Lycidan*). But counter to these runs the most haunting image in the poem, *imminente luna*. A white moon hangs threateningly over spring's rituals.

The fourth is a pattern of light-darkness. The feast of Faunus is a fitting time to celebrate, now in splendor (*nitidum*), now in shadow (*umbrosis*). Death is spoken of as the closing in of *nox* while spring's life-force is presided over by *imminente luna*—which is once again a sort of countercurrent: the rites of spring are held not in the day by sunlight, but at night by the borrowed light of a moon soon to wane (*imminente*). We realize that the countercurrents in all four patterns are there for a reason—the seasons run in a swift and inevitable circle.

The ode is beautifully unified by sounds as well. It is, in fact, a circle of sounds, radiating outward from the four central lines (9-12). It is commonly thought that line 13 is the central point, largely because an exasperated marginal comment of Landor's ("*pallida Mors* has nothing to do with the above"[5]) has sent commentators scurrying to defend the poem's unity, and most of them have accomplished this by magnifying the importance of line 13. Campbell insisted that *pallida Mors* was not only relevant but "the focus of the whole poem," and he has been followed, with more or less emphasis, by Wilkinson, Toll, Rudd, Collinge, Nisbet, and Quinn. Only a few have seen the ode as something other than a 12-8 sonnet-like structure. Sylvester finds both creative and destructive forces in the images of the first three stanzas, so that "thematically, line 13 does not emerge abruptly,"[6] and Commager, noting careful antitheses throughout the ode, regards line 13's abruptness as "more apparent than real."[7] Instead of a two-part ode then, we may find, with Tracy,[8] one steady diminuendo (the outlook progressively narrowing from a panorama of spring to specific incidents in one man's private life) or, as I rather think, what Magariños[9] describes as a contrapuntal structure in the *center* of the poem, extending to the outer stanzas.

Two recent papers regard the central lines (9-12, dealing with the worship of Faunus[10]) as the focus of the poem, Babcock[11] explaining that Faunus is not only guardian of herds but oracular prophet as well, Barr[12] noting that Faunus' festival (February 13) coincides, from the sixth hour, with the *dies parentales*, the festival of the dead. Finally, Heinze[13] considers 9-12 the poem's central link, prepared for in 1-8 and substantiated in 13-20.

Though I do not agree with all Babcock and Barr have to say, I do feel that Faunus, and not *pallida Mors*, is the focus of the poem. From many points of view, 1.4 may be thought of as a circle. It describes the cycle of the seasons in currents and countercurrents of imagery. It is cast in a cyclic rhythm in which the movement of the long dactylo-trochaic line:

–́ ⏕ –́ ⏕ –́ ⏕ –́ ◡◡ ‖ –́ ◡ –́ ◡ –́ ⏓

is reversed in the shorter iambic trimeter catalectic:

⏓ –́ ◡ –́ ⏓ –́ ◡ –́ ◡ –́ ⏓ ∧

There is plainly a thematic cycle—men at work (1-4), Olympian gods (5-8), ceremonies of Faunus (9-12), underworld gods (13-16), men at play (17-20). And the sound waves converge at what must be the ode's focal point, lines 9-12. Let us look first at the long lines:

núnc decet aút viridí nitidúm caput ímpedíre mýrto
núnc et in úmbrosís Faunó decet ímmoláre lúcis.

Nunc echoes *nunc,* and *impedire myrto,* marked off as it is by the strong diaeresis in the line (at the point where dactyls give way to trochees), is answered by the similar-sounding *immolare lucis.*

Moving outwards from the center, we discover that *pede,* rhythmically placed before the diaeresis in line 7, is symmetrically balanced by *pede* in line 13, that *imminente luna* in line 5 parallels *incohare longam* in line 15, and that this last pair echo the trochaic phrases already noted in lines 9 and 11.

A schematization of this will suggest that the sound-patterns form a series of circles with the lines on Faunus at the center:

<table>
<tr><td></td><td></td><td>imminente luna</td></tr>
<tr><td></td><td>pede</td><td></td></tr>
<tr><td>nunc</td><td></td><td>impedire myrto</td></tr>
<tr><td>nunc</td><td></td><td>immolare lucis</td></tr>
<tr><td></td><td>pede</td><td></td></tr>
<tr><td></td><td></td><td>incohare longam</td></tr>
</table>

The opening and closing stanzas seem to have only one common link: the *neque . . . nec* in lines 3 and 4 balanced by the *nec . . . nec* at the beginning of lines 18 and 19. But *within* each of the two stanzas there are patterns. In the concluding stanza, the trochaic *quo simul mearis* is echoed in *quo calet iuventus,* and *et mox* (line 20) balances *-et nox* (in the corresponding position in line 16). Thus the last stanza is connected sonically with the central circle. And at the beginning of the poem, the trochaic clausulae (*veris et Favoni, aut arator igni*) are made to rhyme, while the short iambic lines feature the internal rhyme usually associated with pentameters:

siccas . . . . carinas
canis . . . . pruinis.

This s-pattern is extended into the poem's central section:

Nymphis . . . . decentes
ardens . . . . officinas,

till, at the half-way point, the s-sounds give way to the rhyme

terrae . . . . solutae.[14]

The schema now appears:

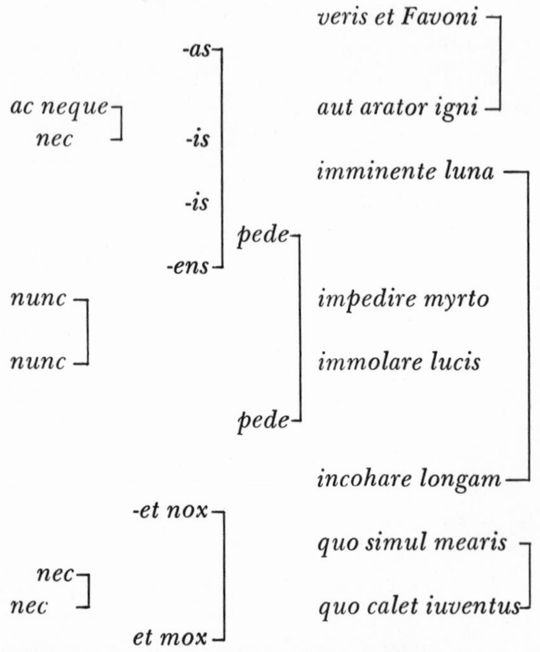

Doubtless there are countercurrents of sound as well. But the overall pattern seems to indicate that Horace composed 1.4 as a thematic and sonic circle with the four lines on Faunus as its center. The ode thus becomes an occasional piece: Horace and Sestius meet to feast and sacrifice in honor of Faunus on his feast day in February,[15] just as the first signs of spring appear on the earth.

2

1.11: WHAT'S IN A NAME?

Tu ne quaesieris (scire nefas) quem mihi, quem tibi
finem di dederint, Leuconoë, nec Babylonios
tentaris numeros. ut melius quidquid erit pati.
seu plures hiemes seu tribuit Iuppiter ultimam,
quae nunc oppositis debilitat pumicibus mare
Tyrrhenum, sapias: vina liques, et spatio brevi
spem longam reseces. dum loquimur, fugerit invida
aetas. carpe diem, quam minimum credula postero.

Please don't try to discern (knowing is wrong)
    what is decreed for me
And for you by the gods, Leuconoë.
    Don't be consulting vast
Chaldee horoscope-books. Better by far
    taking whate'er will be.
If great Jove has ordained more winters still
    or if this be your last
Which now, on the opposed volcanic rocks,
    cripples the Tuscan sea,
you must ever be wise: strain out the wine
    and, as your life is small,
trim luxuriant hope. Now while we speak,
    envious time has passed.
Pluck the flow'r of this day, trusting the next
    little or not at all.

THE MOST STRIKING single feature of this poem is the concise and confident use of the long Asclepiad line, with its marked diaereses after the sixth and tenth syllables. The movement is rapid yet emphatic (Heinze dubs it "energische Knappheit"[1]) so as to reinforce the urgent imperatives. Most of Horace's expressions neatly fill a choriamb: *scire nefas, di dederint, ut melius, quidquid erit, seu tribuit, vina liques, dum loquimur, carpe diem, quam minimum.* The use of single choriambic words is particularly adept: the initial *quaesieris,* the powerful *oppositis debilitat pumicibus* (at least as evocative as Tennyson's "Break, break, break"), and finally, that key word in the poem, the lady's name, Leuconoë.

What's in a name? In an ode of Horace, usually a great deal. Pyrrha's name establishes her role as seductress and destructive force in 1.5; Postumus is "a man born after the death of his father, and hence already launched on the cycle of time that Horace describes"[2] in 2.14; Thaliarchus is part of the pattern of green-youth-spring opposed to white-senility-winter in 1.9; Chloë's name provides the clue to the woodland imagery in 1.23; Horace teases Fuscus about his cognomen by introducing Moorish javelins, the Hydaspes, and the torrid zones into 1.22. The list can easily be extended.[3]

A Leuconoë is mentioned by Hyginus as the daughter of Neptune (157) and consort of Apollo (161), and by Ovid as one of the daughters of Minyas (in *Metamorphoses* 4.168 ff. she tells how Vulcan caught Mars and Venus making love). Undoubtedly the melodious name attracted Horace, always on the lookout for choriambic eighths and sixteenths. But as we expect, he worked its meaning as well as its music into the poem.

What significance does Horace find in λευκὸς νόος? Collinge, with most up-to-date commentators, sees "a Pindaric 'pallid wit' (*Pyth.* 4.109)";[4] the girl is plainly silly, as is evidenced by her compulsive chasing after soothsayers. This reading is not unattractive. 1.11 will then be a companion piece for 1.23: Horace is in love, now with Chloë, now with Leuconoë (*quem mihi, quem tibi finem* shows the mutual regard in 1.11), but in neither poem has he been able to domesticate his distracted mistress. Chloë is afraid to face the sudden springtime of her own maturity, and Leuconoë is given to star-gazing. One timidly clings to the past, the other obsessively peers into the future. Horace's message to both is a predictable, common-sense "live in the present."

But if simple-mindedness were all the name Leuconoë implied, the poem would have to be taken as tongue-in-cheek; the urgent expressions *scire nefas* and *ut melius* would be patronizing, even snide; the winter scene in line 5 would be gratuitous picture-painting; *vina liques* could just as well be an injunction to any household duty—perhaps "tend to your knitting." Small wonder Collinge can only conclude that the poem ends with a "heaping" of "old saws,"[5] that "Horace does no more than say 'carpe diem' in a series of aphorisms piled up in an almost Gilbertian manner."[6] I suspect that Leuconoë's plight *is* similar to Chloë's, that silliness *is* implied in her name. But this is not the whole story by any means.

For Commager, Leuconoë means "clear mind":[7] the girl's one passion is to see into the future. As an interpretation this has undeniable merits: Horace's shocked reaction to the girl's superstition (*scire nefas . . . ut melius*) will not be indulgent persiflage, but Stoic conservatism; the "old saws" will express this disapproval in more characteristically Horatian (i.e. Epicurean) terms; the puzzling *vina liques* will be "opposed to the obscure prophecies of Babylonian astrologers."[8] With Commager the poem is essentially serious. It "might almost be a more explicit redaction of the Soracte Ode":[9] *tu ne quaesieris* echoes *fuge quaerere, vina liques* recalls *benignius . . . deprome merum,* and both poems feature wintry seascapes. But "clear mind" alone will not explain winter's intrusion in 1.11. In fact, it leaves unrelated most of the overtones in the poem's words and images.

As Horace singles out *vina liques* from among all the domestic tasks a peaceful homebody must perform, one is tempted to go Commager one further and read the name as "pure mind": the girl is a pious and innocent miss whose appropriate duty it is to strain wine of its impurities. This will give a still more satisfactory explanation of *scire nefas*: a person who lives *puriter* (as Catullus claims to have done) will want to avoid what is *nefas* and will find positive thinking (*ut melius*) persuasive. In addition, the wintry sea dashed against the rocks can "represent the sinister side of life (pain, trouble, the approach of death) and its effect on the mind."[10] Leuconoë wants the answers to life's mysteries, and Horace suggests that superstitious excesses ill accord with true purity of intention. The difficulty with this reading is that λευκός is not synonymous with, but only suggests, *purus*.

Most simply, Leuconoë means "white mind." And what, we may ask, does "white" mean in Horace's Odes? After the rash of recent exegeses of the Soracte ode it would be unwise to suggest any meaning for "white" which is not connected somehow with "death." In that poem, white, senility, and death are associated motifs, if not all aspects of the same inevitable force. In 1.4, another variant of the *carpe diem* theme, *acris hiems* and *prata albicant* and *pallida Mors* are white pictures which green springtime, for the moment, opposes. It is true that the whiteness of a swan's plume or a girl's shoulder can suggest to Horace other things than death. But winter's white means only one thing. I suspect Leuconoë, who thinks white, is plagued by thoughts of death. If the *finem* at the beginning of line 2 does not imply this, the wintry seascape in line 5 does.

This interpretation will allow the other three to function throughout the poem as well: (4) Leuconoë thinks about death; (3) she is a circumspect, even pious girl, but (2) her obsession drives her to superstitious attempts to clear away her fears and (1) this is silly, for if she could live in the present, Horace might even be able to make love to her. All the associations that cluster about her name are called into play.

The reading "white mind" also affords the richest insight into the poem's imagery. Horace's seascape is made white by specifying the rocks as *pumicibus.* Verrall[11] tries to be even more specific: he cites the very breakwater—the Pontus Julius, completed in 37-36. But this hardly explains the porous volcanic rock Horace introduces into his picture. One rather recalls the Italian film *L'Avventura,* in which white islands of volcanic ash in the *mare Tyrrhenum* are used to symbolize loneliness and isolation. There is no reason to suppose that Horace did not have such bleak and beautiful shapes in mind. But even if we take the traditional explanation (the rocks being gradually eaten away, made porous by the waves' pounding[12]), the image may still be white—and connected with *vina liques,* for the Romans purified their wine by straining it through snow.[13] Sea water slowly eating through white rocks and wine filtered through snow—in both choriambic pictures we have a liquid life-image acting on a white reminder of death. It is difficult to dismiss the intimations of this similarity—and of the difference, which is striking and apposite: in the seascape, the corrosive waves are themselves destroyed on the pumice-rocks, and the three heavy choriambic words suggest that it will always be so; in the filtering process, wine, the symbol of "commitment to present life,"[14] is purified, and the effect of the choriambic phrases is hopefully brisk. While nature's elemental struggle is unending and purposeless, our lives may have some brief meaning.

Horace ends 1.11 with a three-line enjoinder to live in the present. Predictably, his familiar life-images, wine and roses, appear. The concluding lines are no series of "old saws," rattling along like the patter in a lyric Gilbert wrote for Sullivan. If any ghost from the musical theater must be invoked at this point, surely it is Wagner's—the predictable leitmotifs recur, but reshaped and reharmonized masterfully to suit the context: "Leuconoë, you should be putting your house in order; there is wine to be strained, the vine to be pruned; the day has come to full bloom—pluck it now." There is no "heaping" here—only two[15] familiar motifs freshly stated. One might even say the passage is constructed so as *not* to give the impression Collinge draws from it. Notice how Horace's advice has progressed from negative to positive, from perfect subjunctive to present subjunctive to present imperative. Thus gradually and indirectly are we made to feel the increasing urgency. Time is running out. Or rather, as the future perfect *fugerit* indicates, time "will be–has already flown." In addition, *fugerit* colors the next phrase, *carpe diem.* Out of context the familiar tag seems simply a metaphor from pruning; in the context we cannot be quite so sure. Time is some winged thing, and we must catch it while it passes by. Does *fugerit . . . carpe* imply rose or butterfly? There is an almost Empsonian ambiguity about it which Heinze's "Rosen sind ein Symbol der *flüchtigen* Lebensfreude"[16] does nothing to dispel.

Now that we have discussed the interplay of words, sounds, and images in 1.11, we might pause to ask ourselves how valuable such structural analysis is. Does it provide insight into the creative process? Can we see through the poem into the mind and heart of the poet? Can we rehearse the genesis of the ode to Leuconoë?

We can say that Horace found the "commitment to present life" a congenial, even prepossessing theme, and looked about for different ways to express it. *Solvitur acris, Vides ut alta, Persicos odi, Aequam memento,* and *Eheu fugaces* are all distinctive variations, stemming from seasonal, festive, literary, political, and personal experiences. The astrological craze in imperial Rome provided yet another way of treating the theme, and Horace chose to address his poem to one of the gullible. The name Leuconoë may have come from a Greek original, Alcaeus perhaps. In any case it was a happy choice, for not only did it fill a choriamb and so determine the poem's meter, it could imply that the lady was (1) immature, (2) curious to know the future, (3) concerned about living *puriter* and (4) white-minded, i.e., symbolically obsessed with thoughts of death. The gods must dole out this girl's time, not in years, but in winters; the future she seeks to know must be painted white. And though wine and flowers will do, as usual, to represent the present, these can be introduced so that the wine (strained) will reinforce (4) the wintry image and (3) the idea of pure living, while the flowers (pruned) depict (2) the need to cut short future hopes and (1) the importance of living and loving in the present. Content with his ingenuity and armed with a notebook of choriambs (and perhaps a fragment of *Lyra Graeca*), Horace set to work, making the sounds currents, and cross-currents of meaning with the metaphors.

Si fuit ut faceret! All the neat schematization fails absurdly, as it must, when the poem is re-read. Artistic creation is one thing, aesthetic appreciation another. Between the artist and the reader (or listener or performer or critic) stands the art-work itself. We the public have always found subtleties, nuances, relationships which the artist could never have calculated. But then it is our role to appreciate, his to create, and this he must do as his genius moves him. Horace chose his words, rhythms, and images consciously and with great care. It appears that he was able to organize these into significant patterns. But no poet perceives, perhaps no true poet cares to perceive, all the import of his words and pictures as they fall into the metrical molds.

Sometimes the import escapes even the perceptive analyst. Didn't we miss a dominant metaphor in 1.11—from horoscope reading: *finem dederint . . . numeros . . . tribuit . . . plures . . . ultimam . . . spatio brevi . . . diem . . . postero*?

3

1.23: FAUNA AND FLORA

Vitas inuleo me similis, Chloë,
quaerenti pavidam montibus aviis
matrem non sine vano
aurarum et siluae metu.

nam seu mobilibus veris inhorruit
adventus foliis seu virides rubum
dimovere lacertae,
et corde et genibus tremit.

atqui non ego te tigris ut aspera
Gaetulusve leo frangere persequor:
tandem desine matrem
tempestiva sequi viro.

You run from me, Chloë, like a fawn
that seeks her timid dam on pathless mountains,
not without idle fear of the breezes and the forest.

For if the coming of spring has shivered in the
rustling leaves,
or if the green lizards have stirred the bramble bush,
she trembles, both in heart and limb.

And yet, I do not follow you to crush you
like some ferocious tiger or African lion;
so then, stop following your mother.
You're ripe for a man!

HORACE'S ODE TO CHLOË has been thought one of his simpler poems. A century ago, a sensitive translator considered it "trivial."[1] Today the foremost authority on Horace is "hardly inclined to see in it much more than a pretty little artefact."[2] Structural analysts lump it together with a dozen or more odes which are "essentially expansions of a single thought,"[3] wherein "the first part states the situation . . . the second part expresses a contrasting aspect of the same thought."[4] The most recent appraiser detects new subtleties but agrees that Horace "sustains a single tone throughout."[5]

While I do not wish to take serious issue with any of the foregoing, I do think the ode is more interesting and imaginative, structurally, than these verdicts indicate. It is true that the poem's content is easily summarized (the girl is ripe for wooing; she should forget her fears, leave her mother and surrender to her lover), and that this thought is expressed in two unexceptional similes (Horace compares the girl to a fawn[6] but insists he is neither tiger nor lion). The material has been thought commonplace, and for those who have read their way through Diehl and Edmonds this would not be a severe judgment; the similes are clichés from Greek lyric poetry. But the working-out of those similes in 1.23 is remarkable[7] and, from the start, altogether apt: the name of the lady pursued is Chloë (χλόη—a green shoot or twig). Not only the fawn and tiger and lion, but all the woodland images—pathless mountains, breezes, forest, rustling leaves, green lizards, bramble bush —fit naturally and beautifully. And the close

tempestiva[8] . . . *viro*
ripe for a man

is exactly right—a firm reminder for Chloë and, for the reader, a not-too-subtle clue to the pattern of seasonal forest-imagery in the poem.

Chloë's name determines and controls the poem's construction, its emotional level, even the choice of words which make its mosaic. Everything fits neatly. But more than this can be said. Consider the problems that commentators have labored over. *Frangere* seems a strange word to apply to a tiger's onset, and the commentaries outdo themselves in attempts to explain its relevance: "implying desire" (Page), "of crushing between the teeth" (Wickham), "to crunch" (Gow), "mangle" (Botting), "to rend, or tear in pieces, as ἀγνύναι is sometimes employed in Greek" (Anthon).[9] The notorious crux of the poem, however, is *veris inhorruit / adventus foliis,* which Campbell called "a kind of nonsense utterly impossible to Latin, and enough to 'send a shudder' through anybody endowed with some sense of the decencies of Nature, poetry and language."[10] Many texts adopt Bentley's reading *vepris inhorruit / ad ventos,* which is impeccable Latin and eliminates the botanical confusion—for strangely enough, commentators seem less upset by the boldness of the language than by the presence of rustling leaves, lizards, and so forth when spring *arrives.*

I suspect the problems arise through failure to appreciate Horace's not inconsiderable achievement in this poem. He has made use of a simile, standard and readily apparent, in which Chloë *is likened to* a timid fawn; he has at the same time employed throughout a dominant metaphor, derived from the lady's name, in which Chloë *is* a young shoot. The two, simile and metaphor, function simultaneously throughout the poem, from the first line (simile: *inuleo . . . similis;* metaphor: *Chloë*) to the last (simile: *sequi;* metaphor: *tempestiva*). When the fawn-simile is expanded (lines 2-8) the additional details are chosen from the shoot-metaphor (*aviis . . . siluae . . . mobilibus foliis . . . rubum*).

It may be objected that if Chloë is both fawn and foliage, she is afraid of herself. But that is precisely the point: Chloë *is* frightened of her own maturity. "Not without idle fear of wind and woodland" is figurative language for "filled with anxious fears about your own coming of age."

In a poem so imaginatively structured, there seems to be little need to emend, for botanical reasons at least, *veris . . . adventus.* Nature's cycle is, as often in the Odes, our own: the trembling leaves already present for the arrival of spring are Chloë herself, trembling at the advent of new life and love. And *frangere* poses no problem if it applies, not to the tiger/lion-simile, but to the accompanying shoot-metaphor; it hardly suggests an animal attacking, but it fits exactly the snapping of a fragile green twig.

In fact, line 10 may be considered the high point of the poem. It is the climax of the statement, and the point where simile and metaphor all but exceed their limits.

A pretty little poem, surely. But a small *tour de force* as well.

4

1.24: SINGER AND SAINT

Quis desiderio sit pudor aut modus
tam cari capitis? praecipe lugubres
cantus, Melpomene, cui liquidam pater
vocem cum cithara dedit.

ergo Quintilium perpetuus sopor
urget! cui Pudor et Iustitiae soror,
incorrupta Fides, nudaque Veritas
quando ullum inveniet parem?

multis ille bonis flebilis occidit,
nulli flebilior quam tibi, Vergili.
tu frustra pius heu non ita creditum
poscis Quintilium deos.

quid si Threicio blandius Orpheo
auditam moderere arboribus fidem,
num vanae redeat sanguis imagini,
quam virga semel horrida,

non lenis precibus fata recludere,
nigro compulerit Mercurius gregi?
durum: sed levius fit patientia
quidquid corrigere est nefas.

What restraint, what moderation can there be
in our longing for so so well-loved a man as this?
Teach me mournful songs, Melpomene,
you to whom the Father has given a clear voice and
the lyre.

So endless sleep lies on Quintilius!
And Pudor and that sister of Justitia,
Fides undefiled, and naked Veritas
—when will they ever find his like?

He dies mourned by many good men,
but more-to-be-mourned by no one than by you, Virgil.
Piously, but alas in vain, you ask the gods to give
   Quintilius back
—he was not put in your trust on such conditions.

But even if you were to tune the lyre more persuasively
   than Thracian Orpheus
(whose lyre was listened to by trees),
would the blood return to that empty wraith
which Mercury once with shuddery wand

has driven into the black fold?
(He is not moved by prayers to open the gates of death.)
It is hard; but whatever may not be undone
may be made lighter, by Patience.

It is reasonable to suppose that Horace cast his gentle ode on the death of Quintilius Varus in an Asclepiad meter because Quintilius' name nicely fills a choriamb. We might also say that, of all the Muses, Melpomene is singled out, not only for her association with tragedy and elegy, but because of her choriambic name. And while none of the second stanza's virtue-maidens (Pudor, Fides, Veritas) are choriambic, one of them, it seems, has a sister who is—so Horace mentions her (Iustitia). In the myth Horace introduces, Mercurius fits into the metrical scheme, but dactylic Orpheus must be equipped with a specifying choriambic adjective (*Threicio*). Horace has in fact contrived to fill his gentle *Consolatio ad Vergilium* with more than the normal number of self-contained choriambic words: *perpetuus, inveniet, flebilior, arboribus, compulerit.* One wonders why he did not use the name of his addressee, Vergilius, in this way.

Some commentators have been harsh with this melodious threnody. Page says of the first four lines, "I cordially agree with those who wish that Horace had omitted the first stanza, with its weak and affected invocation of the muse, and begun with the bold, vigorous, and effective fifth line, which would have been all the more effective if placed at the beginning of the Ode."[1] But then Walter Savage Landor, savage indeed with the first stanza, will have none of the second either: "What man on such occasion is at leisure to amuse himself with the little plaster images of Pudor and Fides, of Iustitia and Veritas?"[2] As for the rest, R. G. Nisbet, in the most recent comment on the ode, says, "The story about Orpheus and the trees is too fanciful and too trivial for the context."[3] Taken together, these comments would leave nothing of the ode but the last two lines.

It seems to me they have missed the point of the poem —a point made with varying degrees of allusiveness in the two opening stanzas and the references to Orpheus: Horace is giving Virgil Virgilian consolation. The words and images throughout the poem are carefully chosen to speak to Virgil the saint and Virgil the singer of songs. Virtue and poetry, Virgilian ideals, are to be Virgil's comfort. So the two meanings of *modus*: in the first line it is practically synonymous with the *pudor* which accompanies it; it stands for Stoic restraint. But in line 14 (*moderere*) it is used in a musical context; it signifies the proper tuning of the string. Similarly *fides*, a personified virtue in line 7, is a harp-string in line 14. In the indispensable first stanza Melpomene is invoked as a muse divinely endowed with both vocal purity and the lyre. Consider too the three questions Horace asks—the second concerned with virtue, the third with music, the first (*pudor aut modus*) with both. Even the dead man, Quintilius Varus, who is here regarded as companion of the virtues, was poet as well. He appears in the *Ars Poetica* as the grand old man of metrical criticism—outspoken, perceptive, no respecter of persons (hence the appropriateness of the adjectives fixed to his virtues here: *incorrupta Fides nudaque Veritas*). I like to think that this virtuous old master who apprenticed Virgil and Horace was, a generation before, the dissolute young man who took an idle Catullus uptown to see his mistress, i.e., that he was Quintilius Varus from Cremona (a place very much associated with lyre-strings later). The identification is far from certain. But we can be sure that the Varus of the *Ars Poetica* and of the ode under consideration were one and the same, a man practiced in both virtue and poetry.

Have the moral and musical references any special meaning for Virgil?

Two of the virtues singled out for mention, Pudor and Fides, figure in Book IV of the *Aeneid*. Pudor is invoked by Dido at the beginning of the book:

sed mihi vel tellus optem prius ima dehiscat,
vel Pater omnipotens adigat me fulmine ad umbras,
pallentis umbras Erebi noctemque profundam,
ante, Pudor, quam te violo, aut tua iura resolvo
(24-27).

May the earth open and swallow me,
may the almighty Father send me by thunderbolt to the darkness,
to the misty darkness and deepest night of Hell,
before I dishonor thee, Pudor, or break thy laws.

It is Dido's tragedy that her passion for Aeneas undoes this virtue (*solvitque pudorem* 55) and leaves her defenseless (*te propter eundem / extinctus pudor* 321-22). Pudor for Dido means not so much modesty as loyalty to an ideal, in this case loyalty to the memory of a dead husband. And Fides is, for Dido, closely related:

non servata fides cineri promissa Sychaeo! (552)

> I have not kept the *fides* promised my dead
> Sychaeus' ashes!

But the virtue Horace's ode finally recommends, Patientia, is probably the most Virgilian of virtues. Virgil's hero is a man tested and purified by suffering, *multum iactatus,* often counseling patience:

> *O passi graviora, dabit deus his quoque finem*
> (1.199),

> Comrades, you have endured worse sufferings
> —to these too god will put an end,

often counseled to it:

> *quidquid erit, superanda omnis fortuna ferendo est*
> (5.710).

> Whatever will be, we must rise above every turn
> of fate, by bearing it.

The virtues in Horace's ode, then, were not only practiced by the deceased; they were preached by the mourner.

As for the musical references, the myth of Orpheus is surely the heart of the poem. Orpheus, it will be remembered, was both religious leader (the founder of Orphism) and musician. To tell the most beautiful of the many tales which cluster about this legendary figure, we may paraphrase Horace: all nature mourned at the death of Orpheus' bride Eurydice, but no one was more inconsolable than the singer himself; he piously asked the gods to give her back to him, but they put cruel conditions on his trust and his efforts were, alas, in vain. Thus Horace works his way into the myth obliquely, speaking of Orpheus' loss of Eurydice in terms of Virgil's loss of Quintilius:

> *multis ille bonis flebilis occidit,*
> *nulli flebilior quam tibi, Vergili.*
> *tu frustra pius heu non ita creditum*
> *poscis Quintilium deos.*

Asking the gods to give the dead back on terms—so in the third stanza has Horace subtly identified Virgil with Orpheus (too subtly, it seems, for some). In the next stanzas, he makes the point bluntly and explicitly: even if Virgil were capable of the sweet, spell-binding music of Orpheus, he still could not bring life back to an empty wraith Mercury has claimed for death. The modern reader thinks perhaps of Gluck's opera at this point. A Roman would likely remember an Attic frieze widely copied in the Roman world: Orpheus, Eurydice, and Hermes. But Virgil, even in his moment of sorrow, would surely think of a passage in his own work, a passage to which Horace has been directing him from the first—the Orpheus story set at the conclusion of the *Georgics*.

Virgil's fourth *Georgic* discusses in detail the care of bees, the preservation and, at the close, the regeneration of the swarm. Then the four books of didactic poetry end, unexpectedly, with an Alexandrian epyllion. We read the story of Aristaeus, the country god whose swarm was one day touched with infection and died out: Aristaeus runs in tears to his mother Cyrene and then to Proteus, the old man of the sea, for some means to bring his bees back to life, and he is told the myth of Orpheus and Eurydice. At first the Orpheus myth seems out of place in this agricultural context. But apart from the narrative link made by Virgil (it was while fleeing Aristaeus' advances that Eurydice stepped on the serpent that sent her to her death), there are two compelling reasons why Orpheus should be introduced into the poem at this point. First, both Aristaeus and Orpheus attempt to bring the dead back to life. Orpheus is unsuccessful: he looks on Eurydice and loses her forever. Aristaeus is successful: he sacrifices to the shades of Orpheus and Eurydice and from the decaying flesh of his victims his swarm of bees is regenerated. The secrets of life and death are bound up with the rites of Orpheus, who braved the afterlife and all but subdued it by his music. A second, seldom mentioned reason for Orpheus' appearance in the *Georgics* is that it was the legendary Orpheus who first taught man the arts of husbandry, doubtless because by his song he could move all animate creation.[4] Thus Orpheus' civilizing mission in the age of myth is Virgil's in the Augustan age. The Aristaeus and Orpheus myths are relevant to the didactic context of the *Georgics* if they are taken, like the mythology of the *Aeneid,* quasi-allegorically. Aristaeus is "the mythical prototype of the farmer,"[5] and Orpheus is the teacher of agricultural lore. More personally, Aristaeus, seeking knowledge, is the reader of the *Georgics,* while Orpheus, poet and teacher, is the author of the poem. Virgil, descending to Hades in the *Aeneid*[6] and dispensing agricultural lore in the *Georgics,* is the Orpheus of his day. The epyllion may be regarded as his signature to the *Georgics.* In it he identifies himself as Orpheus,[7] even as Cocteau and Rilke were to do in our century.

Horace has this identification in mind in this ode. It is implicit in the third stanza, explicit in the fourth. And the context of the *Georgics* is suggested[8] in several ways. *Auditam . . . arboribus,* far from being trivial, is there to remind the reader that Orpheus had power over the world of nature that Virgil sings of. Horace's line

non lenis precibus fata recludere

seems intended to recall Virgil's

nesciaque humanis precibus mansuescere corda
(4.470)

hearts that do not know how to be moved by
human prayer,

and Horace's Stoic conclusion

durum: sed levius fit patientia
quidquid corrigere est nefas

is a resigned variant of Virgil's more emotional

ignoscenda quidem, scirent si ignoscere Manes
(4.489)

pardonable, surely, if death knew how to pardon.

1.24: Singer and Saint

It is often said that the Orpheus section of the *Georgics* is Virgil's finest single episode. Surely, of the mature writings, it comes closest to being a personal statement. It hardly seems likely that Virgil would have thought the tender, allusive use of Horace made of it "affected" or "trivial." Rather, he must have been both complimented and consoled by the reminder that his own dedication was, like Quintilius' and like Orpheus', twofold: to virtue and to poetry.

5

1.38: THIRST FOR LIFE

Persicos odi, puer, apparatus,
displicent nexae philyra coronae;
mitte sectari, rosa quo locorum
sera moretur.

simplici myrto nihil allabores
sedulus curo: neque te ministrum
dedecet myrtus neque me sub arta
vite bibentem.

My lad, I hate Persian pomp.
Garlands woven on linden bark offend me.
Stop searching through all the places where
the late rose may linger.

My special care is that you add nothing,
in your labors, to simple myrtle. Myrtle disgraces
neither you as you serve nor me as I
drink beneath the trellised vine.

Persicos odi is the last poem in Book I. It is strategically placed. Its Sapphic stanzas reply to the Alcaics of the preceding poem, *Nunc est bibendum* (and this antiphony will be the prevailing pattern in Book II[1]); its quiet tone dissipates the frenzied enthusiasm of the previous ode (both are drinking songs, but the former's *nunc est bibendum* is transmuted in the latter to a leisurely *vite bibentem*); and its theme—the rejection of Oriental luxury in favor of

Roman simplicity—eases the passage from Cleopatra who precedes to Cato and the civil wars which follow. This is a prime instance of *callida iunctura,* not of words within a poem but of poems within the corpus.

But one hesitates to take *Persicos odi* too seriously. If the odes which conclude the other books are parallel cases, it might be an elaborate leg-pull.[2] Book II concludes with Horace's grotesque metamorphosis into a swan as he prepares to sing the Roman Odes,[3] and Book III ends with *Exegi monumentum,* a self-tribute so stupendous that of late it has been called "diffident" if not mock-serious.[4] Similarly, Book I ends with *Persicos odi,* a rejection of luxury in which "the rose lingers in our memory longer than Horace's rejection of it."[5]

Encouraged, then, by Horace himself to take the ode with tongue at least partially in cheek, I should like to call attention to a striking bit of parallelism which may give a clue to the meaning of this thought-teasing epilogue. Page has noticed that *apparatus* in the first line is balanced by *allabores* in the corresponding position in stanza two; the words are not only metrically equivalent but sound alike, and "the *ad* in both words suggests the idea of excess."[6] In addition, there is metrical equivalence (and contrast) in the initial *Persicos* and the corresponding word in stanza two, *simplici* (though there is little assonance here). One might find some amusement and perhaps even profit comparing the corresponding words in the two stanzas throughout, seeking what Collinge calls the "balance of content parallel to the metrical correspondences of the formal Greek style."[7] If this is done, the best effect is saved for last, and rightly so, for in the Sapphic stanza we expect the concluding short line, the adonic, to linger longest in the memory. The adonics in this poem are *sera moretur* and *vite bibentem.*

These melodious phrases sum up their stanzas; Horace may be contrasting rose and myrtle, but metrically it is *sera moretur* he rejects and *vite bibentem* he asks for. If the rose and the vine are recurrent life-images in Horace, this is especially true in the predominantly somber book of odes which follows *Persicos odi.*[8] Our days on earth are, for Horace, days of wine and roses:

> *huc vina et unguenta et nimium breves*
> *flores amoenae ferre iube rosae*
>
> (2.3.13-14).

> Bid them bring here wines and perfumes
> and the too-brief blossoms of the lovely
> rose.

But as the Epicurean finds to his dismay, amid the cups and chaplets *surgit amari aliquid*—some bitter reminder wells up to spoil the fragrance of the flowers.[9] The roses, in Horace, are *nimium breves* or *serae*; the wine will be spilled on the pavement by some worthier heir. Roses "sind ein Symbol der *flüchtigen* Lebensfreude";[10] wine "represents a commitment to *present* life."[11] There is a difference worth noting here. The rose fades and dies, as we ourselves must inevitably do. But wine can be stored away in cellars, preserved and guarded with a hundred keys; we may die without enjoyment of it, and it will keep its sweetness for someone who knows how to live in the present. So when Horace dissociates his two life-images in *Persicos odi,* rejecting one and demanding the other, it is as if the rose has become for him a reminder of death.

If *Todesablehnung* seems out of place in a half-serious epilogue, it might be noted that the odes which close the other books contain similar sentiments. 2.20 ends with a (mock serious?) rejection of death-symbols:

> *absint inani funere neniae*
> *luctusque turpes et querimoniae;*
> *compesce clamorem ac sepulcri*
> *mitte supervacuos honores*
>
> (21-24).

> As I'll not be there for my funeral, let there
> be no dirges sung, and no disgraceful expres-
> sions of grief and lamentation. Stifle your

> sobs, and never mind the worthless tribute of
> a tomb.

And 3.30 has

> *non omnis moriar, multaque pars mei*
> *vitabit Libitinam*
>
> (6-7).
>
> I shall not altogether die, no—a great part
> of me will escape the death-Venus.

Can the life-image Horace rejects in 1.38 be associated with death? Possibly, for in addition to the sober Epicurean overtones in *sera moretur,* there is something about the sound of that late-blooming rose: the change from *sera moretur* to *sera morietur* requires the addition of only one letter. A suspicion that here Horace might intend more than meets the ear is only strengthened when we note that, in the contrasting, affirmative adonic of the second stanza, it is almost a matter of mere phonetics to pass from *vite bibentem* to *vita viventem.*[12]

This need not be mere aural association or Jabberwocky nonsense. Horace seems nowhere else to resort to portmanteau words, but there are similar sound-patterns in Lucretius, and while some editors deplore these as unworthy puns, Paul Friedländer has dignified them with the term "atomology."[13] Lucretius himself notes the connection, naturally and orthographically, between *ligna* and *ignis*:

> *nonne vides igitur . . .*
> *. . . eadem paulo inter se mutata creare*
> *ignis et lignum? quo pacto verba quoque ipsa*
> *inter se paulo mutatis sunt elementis,*
> *cum ligna atque ignis distincta voce notemus*
>
> (1.911-14).
>
> Haven't you noticed . . . that the same atoms,
> with only a slight change in composition,
> can make fire and wood? Why, the very words

> themselves, when we say *ligna* and *ignis*, are
> only slightly different.

Doubtless most instances of this in Lucretius are playful, but Bailey concludes "the fundamental idea is sound and goes far to explain arguments in the poem which might otherwise appear puerile."[14]

"Atomology" of words may or may not be a trade-mark of the playful Epicurean poet. But I suspect a trace of it in *Persicos odi* where Horace is speaking as an Epicurean and (in a closing ode) being playful as well. Literally he rejects Oriental luxury for Italian simplicity; perhaps alliteratively he is also bidding farewell to a lingering *memento mori* and calling his slave boy to come fill the cup of life.[15]

6

2.3 AND 2.14: DAYS OF WINE AND ROSES

Aequam memento rebus in arduis
servare mentem, non secus in bonis
ab insolenti temperatam
laetitia, moriture Delli,

seu maestus omni tempore vixeris,
seu te in remoto gramine per dies
festos reclinatum bearis
interiore nota Falerni.

quo pinus ingens albaque populus
umbram hospitalem consociare amant
ramis? quid obliquo laborat
lympha fugax trepidare rivo?

huc vina et unguenta et nimium breves
flores amoenae ferre iube rosae,
dum res et aetas et sororum
fila trium patiuntur atra.

cedes coemptis saltibus et domo
villaque, flavus quam Tiberis lavit;
cedes, et exstructis in altum
divitiis potietur heres.

divesne prisco natus ab Inacho
nil interest an pauper et infima
de gente sub divo moreris,
victima nil miserantis Orci.

omnes eodem cogimur, omnium
versatur urna serius ocius
sors exitura et nos in aeternum
exsilium impositura cumbae.

Remember to keep an even mind, one restrained
from excessive joy in adversity and likewise
in prosperity, Dellius, doomed to die!

Whether you live in sadness all your days
or whether, reclining on some sequestered
lawn, you take delight through the holidays
in some choice brand of Falernian.

Why do the towering pine and white poplar
love to make friendly shade together with
their branches? Why does the rushing water
struggle to hurry down the winding river course?

Bid them bring here wines and perfumes and the
too-brief blossoms of the lovely rose, while the
world and time allow it, and the dark thread of
the three sisters.

You will leave your purchased woodlands and
your home and your villa, which the yellow Tiber
washes; and you will leave them, and an heir will
take possession of your riches, heaped on high.

It matters not whether you linger under the open
sky a rich man, descended from ancient Inachus,
or a poor man and from the lowest stock; you
are a victim of Orcus who knows no pity.

We are all being herded to the same end;
the lot of every man is tossing in the urn,
destined soon or late to leap out and place us,
for everlasting exile, on the skiff.

THE PATTERN OF IMAGES in this ode seems to fit the second of the classifications made by H. L. Tracy: interwoven themes. One detects "two thematic ideas intertwined, and these form almost the entire material of the poem."[1] 2.3 is one of Horace's finest statements of Epicurean thought, for its somewhat predictable themes, the sweetness of life and the inevitability of death, are made memorable not only by the images used to express them but by the interweaving of those images.

We have noted that the sweetness of life is most characteristically expressed by Horace in terms of wine and roses. In 2.3 these patterns occur, but for more varied effect they are expanded to include other liquid and vegetative images: life is represented in sensuous terms, either of wine, water, and ointment, or of roses, grass, and trees.

Interwoven with these are death-images, ranging from the mythological and straightforward (the thread of the Fates, unpitying Orcus, Necessity's urn and Charon's boat) to the powerfully suggestive (*sub divo moreris / victima* suggests the sacrificial animal let out to pasture one last day before the slaughter,[2] and *omnes eodem cogimur* suggests Mercury herding the shades[3]) to the deliberately emphatic (*moriture Delli*). We also expect that "triumphant reminder of time passing,"[4] the heir, to loom up somewhere in the poem; he is the one death-image Horace has made virtually his own.

How has Horace arranged and orchestrated his many leitmotifs? He begins his poem with what seems to be a deliberately prosaic statement of Epicurean doctrine; all the emphasis in the first stanza is thus reserved for that startling *moriture,* aimed at Dellius the opportunist-millionaire. This first death-motif is sounded, as it were, *fortissimo* at the close of the stanza.

In the second stanza, the sweet life (as opposed to *maestus*) is pictured in terms vegetative (*gramine*) and liquid (*Falerni*).

In the third stanza, Horace asks his rhetorical questions: "Why the lovely shade trees?" and "Why the rippling stream?" However we reply, the images are once more carefully chosen according to pattern, one vegetative, one liquid.

Horace's own answer to the questions is a determination to live while he may, and in the fourth stanza he calls for wine and ointment, and the blossoms of the rose. But these life-images are followed by the second reminder of death (*fila . . . atra*) at the close of the stanza.

As death is a departure from living, the life-images in the fifth stanza represent what Dellius must leave behind: his groves and his Tiber-washed villa. But again the vegetative and liquid images are followed by a reminder of death—the heir.

From here to the end of the poem, life-images are halted. The thought of the sixth stanza (rich or poor, you must die) is commonplace, but the images (the *victima* in the field, *nil miserantis Orci*) are particularly grim.

Finally the death-images close in completely. Collinge describes the last stanza as a "relentlessly moving description of the descent to the exile of death."[5] The images here are three (*cogimur*, Necessity's urn and Charon's boat), and there are echoes of *moriture* in *exitura . . . impositura.*

As in some symphonic movement, the death-theme, unforgettably sounded at the beginning of the ode, is only intermittently displaced by a twofold life-theme; death gathers momentum, sounding in the final line of three stanzas, to triumph completely at the close. This pattern might be schematized thus:

st. 1	*moriture*	
st. 2		*gramine* *Falerni*
st. 3		*pinus . . . populus* *lympha*
st. 4		*flores . . . rosae* *vina et unguenta*
	fila . . . atra	
st. 5		*saltibus* *Tiberis*
	heres	
st. 6	*victima* *nil miserantis Orci*	

st. 7 *cogimur*
urna
cumbae
exitura . . . impositura

To say this much, however, is still to miss the subtlest aspect of 2.3. Let us pause to look briefly at another ode, with a similar theme—2.14:

Eheu fugaces, Postume, Postume,
labuntur anni nec pietas moram
rugis et instanti senectae
adferet indomitaeque morti:

non si trecenis quotquot eunt dies,
amice, places illacrimabilem
Plutona tauris, qui ter amplum
Geryonen Tityonque tristi

compescit unda, scilicet omnibus,
quicumque terrae munere vescimur,
enaviganda, sive reges
sive inopes erimus coloni.

frustra cruento Marte carebimus
fractisque rauci fluctibus Hadriae,
frustra per autumnos nocentem
corporibus metuemus Austrum:

visendus ater flumine languido
Cocytos errans et Danai genus
infame damnatusque longi
Sisyphus Aeolides laboris:

linquenda tellus et domus et placens
uxor, neque harum quas colis arborum
te praeter invisas cupressos
ulla brevem dominum sequetur:

absumet heres Caecuba dignior
servata centum clavibus et mero
tinget pavimentum superbo,
pontificum potiore cenis.

Alas Postumus, Postumus, the fleeting years
are slipping past, and all your virtuous ways
will not stave off wrinkles and advancing age
and unconquered death—

no my friend, not if you were to avert the anger
of tearless Pluto with three hundred bulls each
day that passes. For he imprisons Geryon, three
times your size, and Tityus too,

with that gloomy stream that all of us, you
may be sure, must sail across—all of us who
eat the fruits of earth, though we be kings or
poor country folk.

In vain shall we keep clear of bloody Mars and
the roaring Adriatic's crashing waves; in vain
through the autumn season shall we fear the South
Wind which brings disease to our bodies.

You must look upon black Cocytus with its sluggish
waters, and the infamous daughters of Danaus, and
Aeolus' son, Sisyphus, condemned to unending labor.

You must leave your land and home and loving wife,
and of these trees you tend, none will follow you,
their short-lived master, save the hated cypresses.

A worthier heir will take possession of your
Caecuban wines, guarded with a hundred keys,
and stain the pavement with the proud vintage,
more than fit for priestly feasts.

Here it is Postumus who is addressed, "a man," Commager remarks, "born after the death of his father, and hence already launched on the cycle of time that Horace describes."[6] There is no need to direct a *moriture* at this all-but-anonymous mortal. In 2.14, death-images from mythology parade past in swift succession (Pluto, the Cocytus, imprisoned Geryon and Tityus, the daughters of Danaus, Sisyphus) and the heir takes over relentlessly at the end.

The tone of the ode is almost unrelievedly gloomy—yet we notice that it too is filled with liquid and vegetative images. The important difference is that these no longer group together as a life-theme in counterpoint to a death-theme. In 2.14, death's influence is pervasive and thorough: *even the liquid and vegetative images are death images.* Words usually associated with water in Horace, *fugaces* and *labuntur,* here describe the inevitable passing of time; *unda* signifies the prison of death; we avoid *cruento Marte* and *fluctibus Hadriae,* liquid harbingers of death; death means gazing on black Cocytus with its *flumine languido,* and on the daughters of Danaus, endlessly filling their pitchers with water; the ultimate irony is not so much the heir coming into his own as his splashing wine on the pavement.[7] As for vegetative imagery, mortals are described as *quicumque terrae munere vescimur;*[8] we avoid the *Austrum* which, in Augustan poetry, is associated with the destruction of trees and crops in the autumn season;[9] death means leaving not only house and wife (Lucretius had already said as much), but trees as well—all but the hated cypress.[10]

If Horace's sensuous life-images can be so ruthlessly used in 2.14[11] to symbolize death as well, one wonders how correct we are in identifying them in 2.3 simply as images of life. Returning to that poem, then, we note how Horace has been careful to qualify his life-images. Each is accompanied by a word which might appear at first curious, even otiose, but which actually colors and darkens the image: the lawn is *remoto*; the brand of Falernian is *interiore*; pine and poplar embrace to form an *umbram*; the water in the rippling stream is *fugax*; the roses are *nimium breves*; the groves are only *coemptis* and must be surrendered, as must the villa lapped by a river which is ominously *flavus.*[12] There is something withdrawn or impermanent or sinister about the very symbols of life, *even while they are being enjoyed.*

Death's influence pervades 2.3 just as surely as it does 2.14. But the tone is subtler. This, I suspect, is why the key word at the beginning of 2.3 is not *mortalis* but the more dynamic *moriture*. Living we die, and the loveliest symbols of life can only remind us of this. Perhaps Lucretius wrote the best commentary on 2.3 in advance when he said:

> *pocula crebra, unguenta coronae serta parantur,*
> *nequiquam, quoniam medio de fonte leporum*
> *surgit amari aliquid quod in ipsis floribus angat*
> (4.1132-34).

> Goblets, scents, woven chaplets are made ready
> in profusion—all useless, for something bitter
> wells up from the source of the fountain of
> pleasures, amid the very flowers, and this
> brings grief.

7

3.9: DUETTINO AL RICERCARE

Donec gratus eram tibi
nec quisquam potior bracchia candidae
cervici iuvenis dabat,
Persarum vigui rege beatior.

donec non alia magis
arsisti neque erat Lydia post Chloën,
multi Lydia nominis
Romana vigui clarior Ilia.

me nunc Thraessa Chloë regit,
dulces docta modos et citharae sciens,
pro qua non metuam mori,
si parcent animae fata superstiti.

me torret face mutua
Thurini Calaïs filius Ornyti,
pro quo bis patiar mori,
si parcent puero fata superstiti.

quid si prisca redit Venus
diductosque iugo cogit aëneo?
si flava excutitur Chloë
reiectaeque patet ianua Lydiae?

quamquam sidere pulchrior
ille est, tu levior cortice et improbo
iracundior Hadria,
tecum vivere amem, tecum obeam libens.

HE As long as I was loved by you,
And you allowed no other boy to throw
His arms around your snow-white neck,
I lived a richer man than Persia's king.

SHE As long as you burned just for me,
And Lydia didn't serve in Chloë's train,
I, Lydia, had a mighty name
And lived more famed than Ilia of Rome.

HE Now Thracian Chloë rules my heart;
She's taught to sing sweet tunes and play the lute,
And for her I'd not fear to die,
If fate would spare my love and let her live.

SHE Now Calaïs from Thurian stock
Sets me ablaze with passion he returns,
And for him I'd twice gladly die,
If fate would spare my lad and let him live.

HE What if our former love revived,
And Venus locked us in a yoke of bronze?
If Chloë were cast out of doors,
And long-rejected Lydia taken in?

SHE Well—he's more lovely than a star,
And you are light as cork, and just as mad
As th' Adriatic in a storm—
But still I'd gladly live and die with you.

"I WOULD RATHER have composed odes like these than be king of all Aragon." Scaliger[1] goes too far. There are no odes like this one. Nowhere else has Horace placed words and sounds antiphonally to such excellent effect:

donec	*donec*
Persarum vigui	*Romana vigui*
me . . . Thraessa Chloë	*me . . . Thurini Calaïs*

pro qua . . . mori	*pro quo . . . mori*
si parcent . . . fata superstiti	*si parcent . . . fata superstiti*
qu*id* si pr*isca*	qu*amquam* sid*ere* pul*chrior*

The lovers' quarrel lasts as long as stanza echoes stanza, and ends when antiphonal balance is established within the line:

tecum vivere amem, tecum obeam libens.

Tecum echoes *tecum*; in sense *obeam* answers *vivere* and *amem* corresponds to *libens*, but in sound the two pairs of words (like the two pairs of lovers) should be rematched, and *amem* made to go with *obeam*, *vivere* with *libens*. The assonance in this line is remarkable, and one is conscious of alliteration throughout the poem: *candidae cervici, dulces docta, metuam mori, parcent puero, improbo iracundior.*

The poem's images are likewise balanced and contrasted. Both lovers have sought out gentler company: Her Calaïs of Thurii is, by name and place of origin,[2] devoted to pleasure, even effeminate, while his Thracian Chloë is not, as her name would indicate, a wild woodland sprite—she is sweet, cultivated, musically accomplished. We infer that the speakers themselves are of sturdier cast, and their language bears this out. He thinks of love as rule by force (*regit; iugo cogit aëneo*) in brusquely physical terms (*bracchia . . . dabat*; *excutitur*); she sees it as flame (*arsisti*; *torret face*) and her comparisons are imaginative (*sidere pulchrior*; *levior cortice*; *iracundior Hadria*).

Every word adds a fresh detail. We can almost reconstruct the history of the spat. He all but admits having started it (*reiectae . . . Lydiae*); she agrees (*tu . . . iracundior*), implying he was the first to cast his eyes elsewhere (*levior*). He seems thereafter to have fallen completely from her favor (*donec gratus eram*); she still claims second place in his affections (*alia magis*; *Lydia post Chloën*).

But the point of amoebean verse is that each statement must be answered in similar terms and somehow capped. So while the anonymous boy is at first reluctant to mention his rival's name, and resorts to a vague *quisquam potior,* the girl speaks explicitly of the Chloë who has replaced her, names herself, and then parries his *Persarum vigui* with *Romana vigui.* The word-placing calls *Persicos odi* unmistakably to mind. We may hesitate to identify the boy as Horace himself until we reach line eight and spot the antithesis. Then we see that the boy loses the first round only if he is the author of 1.38. He has no business using the king of Persia as an example of his *beatitudo* when he has officially rejected all such oriental grandipotence. Her *Romana,* then, is the perfect answer—especially as it comes from a lady who prides herself on her eastern connections: *multi Lydia nominis.*

Horace tries a new approach in round two. Moving from old love to new, from past to present and future, from memories of happy living to thoughts of dying for love, he sings of his current enslavement to a cultured Greek miss for whom he would not fear to die. Lydia caps this with conspicuous ease: she is no slave; her lover loves her on an equal level. What's more he is a sybarite from the very lap of luxury—in Italy. And far from being afraid to die for him, she would gladly offer herself to suffering and death—twice. A few adroit changes, and Horace's very words are turned against him.

Horace realizes he is no match for Lydia (cf. the "bronze yoke," explained in 1.33.10-12 as Venus' means of mating the *impares*). He decides to make up as best he can, and his offer is made as much in word-patterns as in words. His statements no longer challenge her to reply in turn; they double back on themselves: *di-ductos* is reversed in *co-git, excutitur* in *patet ianua.* Lydia picks up the clue. After an alliterative attempt to cap Horace, she makes a few invidious comparisons[3] and then surrenders, in as nicely turned a line as our poet ever achieved:

tecum vivere amem, tecum obeam libens.

Apart from its verbal and aural refinements, the line

neatly rephrases the living of the first exchange (*vigui . . . vigui*), the dying of the second (*mori . . . mori*). The themes are restated with the discord resolved.

This may be the crowning irony of the poem. Lydia's capitulation caps everything that went before. Like the close of a musical movement in sonata form, it is *re*capitulation.

So the constituent words, sounds, and images of 3.9 are related, juxtaposed, balanced to maximum effect. The poem is sometimes dismissed as an overstylized imitation of earlier poems in the amoebean genre; it may be more properly viewed as an intensification of Horace's own lyric technique —antithetic, architechtonic, imaginative. And unfeeling? On the polished surface of this poem, there is no display of emotion at all. But how eminently right this is, for the most impressive feat of balance in all the acrobatics of 3.9 is that Horace has put himself in the poem and has yet contrived to remain outside it, the omniscient lyricist in a moment of self-satire.

Horace's purpose is not so much to communicate emotion as to shape it. Like any artist, he strives to put specially intensified experiences into the only possible forms which (for him) will convey them to his listener. Even the straightforward Catullus once cast his affair with Lesbia in formal pseudonymous patterns—and his forty-fifth poem is the only duettino that even bears comparison with *Donec gratus eram.*

NOTES

Part I

NOTES TO CHAPTER 1

1. The Horatian stanza is more properly a strophe (turn) inherited from those Greek lyricists (Sappho and Alcaeus) who wrote poems in metrically identical units, rather than from those (Pindar, Bacchylides) who wrote in the more elaborate pattern strophe–antistrophe–epode. The stanza is a modern development of the strophe. But the terms are often used interchangeably. See, for example, Jacques Perret, *Horace* (New York, 1964), pp. 70-80. August Meineke first demonstrated that the total number of lines in any ode of Horace (including 4.8) is divisible by four.
2. Gilbert Norwood, *Pindar* (Berkeley, 1945), esp. pp. 98-164.

NOTES TO CHAPTER 2

1. In the *Ars Poetica* and other literary epistles, Horace writes as critic, not as practitioner revealing the secrets of the trade. It is, however, reasonable to suppose he would expect his dicta to apply to his own lyric poetry, even *mutatis mutandis* those dicta which strictly apply to epic and drama.
2. *Götzendämmerung*: Was ich den Alten Verdanke, 1.
3. See, for example, N. E. Collinge, *The Structure of Horace's Odes* (Oxford, 1961), p. 2.
4. Quoted in Cleanth Brooks, *The Well Wrought Urn* (New York, 1947), p. 9.
5. From the last of the *Four Quartets.*
6. See p. 38.
7. See, for example, L. P. Wilkinson, *Golden Latin Artistry* (Cambridge, 1963), p. 220, and Ernest A. Fredricksmeyer, "Horace's Ode to Pyrrha," *CP* 60 (1965), p. 183.
8. From the preface to *Sylvae.*

9. H. D. Naylor (*Horace, Odes and Epodes* [Cambridge, 1922], pp. xiv-xv, § 7) lists 12 instances of the chiastic, 15 of the achiastic type.
10. For further examples, see Naylor, *op. cit.*, p. xxii, § 33.
11. For a fairly complete list, see Naylor, *op. cit.*, p. xxx, § 52.
12. This was first suggested by Collinge, *op. cit.*, p. 32.
13. Giorgio Pasquali, *Orazio Lirico* (Florence, 1918).
14. Several other odes of Horace show no discernible borrowing, but are very much in the style of Pindar (1.7 and 4.4), Stesichorus (1.16), the dithyrambic poets (2.19 and 3.25), and the Hellenistic epigrammatists (1.30 and 3.22). Tenney Frank (*Catullus and Horace* [New York, 1928], pp. 232-39) suggests that Horace used the mottoes to help the literate Roman identify the meter.
15. Cf. *ponto nox incubat atra* (1.89) and, from the related *incumbo, incubuere mari* (1.84) and *angues / incumbunt pelago* (2.205). Though the odes were published four years before the *Aeneid,* 1.3 could easily have followed the composition of the first books of the *Aeneid,* which was ten years in the writing. Indeed there is a strong tradition for placing 1.3 among the latest of the odes; see Wickham's edition (Oxford, 1877), *ad loc.* For Virgilian echoes in 1.24 see *infra,* Part II, chapter 4; on 4.12, see C. M. Bowra, "Horace, *Odes* IV, 12," *CR.* 42 (1928), pp. 165-67.
16. Parts of the introduction to Book II of Lucretius are refashioned in Book II of the Odes. Cf. Lucr. 2.27 and Horace 2.18.1-2; Lucr. 2.28 and Horace 2.16.11-12; Lucr. 2.29-33 and Horace 2.3.4-12. These Lucretian themes are forcefully restated in Horace 3.1.13-24.
17. Kenneth Quinn (*Latin Explorations* [London, 1963], pp. 99-108) sees the Lucretian echo as a clue to the form of the ode: a dramatic monologue, table-talk such as Lucretius mentions in 3.912-15. Thomas Gray also remembered Lucretius in the sixth stanza of the *Elegy*:

    For them no more the blazing hearth shall burn,
    Or busy housewife ply her evening care.
18. Compare Lucretius 1.6-15: *te fugiunt venti . . . tibi suavis daedala tellus / summittit flores . . . species patefactast verna diei . . . rapidos tranant amnis.*
19. Compare Lucretius 5.737-47. But note too that the startlingly placed *et mox* also occurs in Odes 1.4.20, balanced by *-et nox*

in line 16 there. One thinks of the *-et nox* in Catullus 7.7 and the use of *lux / nox* in Catullus 5.5-6.

20. *The Classical Tradition in Poetry* (rep. New York, 1957), p. 151.
21. Marginal glosses made by Walter Savage Landor, quoted in A. Y. Campbell, *Horace, A New Interpretation* (London, 1924), p. 8.
22. See *Epistles* 2.2.115-19 and *Ars Poetica* 60-72.
23. *Op. cit.*, p. 8.
24. *Ibid.*, p. 210.
25. Other notable instances are *pinus ingens albaque populus* (2.3.9), *gelidos . . . rubro sanguine rivos* (3.13.6-7), and another passage in the Soracte ode (1.9.21-22), which has received a glowing tribute from Murray, *op. cit.*, p. 150. Petronius' two-word summary of Horace's style, *curiosa felicitas,* is itself an instance of *callida iunctura.* So too Quintilian's verdict, *verbis felicissime audax.*
26. See A. Y. Campbell, *op. cit.*, p. 224, and Eduard Fraenkel, *Horace*, pp. 176-77. The defense, led by L. P. Wilkinson (*Horace andHis Lyric Poetry* [Cambridge, 1945], pp. 129-31), crested in the late 1950's: H. C. Toll, "Unity in the Odes of Horace," *Phoenix* 9 (1955), esp. pp. 162-63; M. P. Cunningham, "*Enarratio* of Horace *Odes* 1.9," *CP* 52 (1957), pp. 98-102; M. G. Shields, "*Odes* 1.9: A Study in Imaginative Unity," *Phoenix* 12 (1958), pp. 166-73; E. M. Blaiklock, "The Dying Storm," *Greece and Rome* 6 (1959), esp. pp. 208-9; N. Rudd, "Patterns in Horatian Lyric," *AJP* 81 (1960), pp. 373-92.
27. In Epode 13.4-5 *virent genua,* contrasted with *senectus,* indicates a similar pattern. In 2.11.6-8 *levis iuventas* is contrasted with *arida canitie.*
28. *Latin Poetry* (London, 1895), p. 206.
29. "Squares and Oblongs," in *Poets at Work* (New York, 1948), p. 171.

NOTES TO CHAPTER 3

1. See *De Structura Orationis,* 14. The sounds and rhythms of Latin verse are discussed in L. P. Wilkinson, *Golden Latin Artistry* (hereafter referred to as *GLA*), an indispensable study to which this chapter is heavily indebted.

2. *Orator* 68, 162-63.
3. "Rhythm and Rhyme" (1918), reprinted in *Poets on Poetry,* ed. Charles Norman (New York, 1962), pp. 322-23.
4. *GLA,* p. 31.
5. Cf. also 1.3.28-29; 2.4.4-5; 3.3.60-61; 3.16.15; 4.2.14-15 and 4.8.11.
6. Cf. also 1.13.1-2; 1.35.15; 3.3.18; 3.26.6; 4.1.2; 4.2.49-50 and 4.4.70.
7. Is the ode to Barine (2.8) a hymn in reverse? Horace declares himself a non-believer (*si fieres turpior, crederem*), and the prayer formula of the last stanza (*te . . . te . . . tua*) is preceded by other formal groups of three: *cineres, signa, divos; Venus, Nymphae, Cupido; pubes, servitus, priores.*
8. *Asphodel* (1949), p. 13.
9. I have treated Catullus' use of elision in "Illustrative Elisions in Catullus," *TAPA* 93 (1962), pp. 144-53.
10. The line is, like Hercules, rough-and-ready: the elision prevents diaeresis, and the last syllable of *perrupit* must be lengthened by verbal stress.
11. *The Classical Tradition in Poetry* (hereafter referred to as *TCTIP*) p. 83.
12. See *Ars Poetica* 441-46.
13. See *Ars Poetica* 73-86.
14. Alexander Pope, *An Essay on Criticism,* part two.
15. *TCTIP,* p. 71.
16. *TCTIP,* p. 104.
17. "The Music of Poetry" (1942), in *On Poetry and Poets* (New York, 1961), p. 20. A similar phenomenon occurs in Gregorian chant, where there is a constant interplay of musical and verbal stresses.
18. A famous example:

    Íste conféssor Dómini, coléntes
    quém pie laúdant pópuli per órbem,
    hác die laétus méruit beátas
      scándere sédes.

19. 4.6 seems to have been written on the occasion of Horace's commission to write the *Carmen Saeculare.* In lengthening *syllabae ancipites* and observing caesurae Horace was regularizing what was already a marked tendency in the Greek. Denys Page (*Sappho and Alcaeus* [Oxford, 1955], p. 324) notes that the fourth syllable is long two-thirds of the time

in Sappho's fragments, with the break after the fifth syllable occurring "in about five-eighths of the instances."

20. Note that the uxorious river has metrically overflowed into the adonic. Other instances of such interlinear word-division are 1.25.11 and 2.16.7.
21. *GLA*, p. 107.
22. Cf. lines 7, 9, 13, 17, 23, 33, 34, 38, 41, 47, 49, and 50.
23. Like the Sapphic, Asclepiad meters were later converted from quantitative to accentual, e.g.,

    Pánis angélicus fít panis hóminum,
    dát panis caélicus fíguris términum;
    Ó res mirábilis! mánducat Dóminum
      paúper, sérvus et húmilis.

24. *TCTIP*, pp. 100-101.
25. Horace was, again, normalizing what was fairly common practice in Alcaeus, who observed the pause after the fifth syllable about two-thirds of the time. See Page, *Sappho and Alcaeus*, p. 323.
26. *GLA*, pp. 110-11.
27. It might almost be said that in the third and fourth lines in every stanza of 1.34 (wherein Horace "backslides"), the sound *and sense* tack about and retrace their course. This effect may not have been original with Horace. At least two passages in the fragments of Alcaeus show a similar accommodation of sound to sense: 298.12-13 LP as restored by Page, *Sappho and Alcaeus*, p. 283 (δ' ἄιξε πόν]τον, ἐκ δ' ἀφάντοις / αἶψ ἀνέμω]ν ἐκύκα θυέλλαις) and 326.3-4 LP (τὸ δ' ἔνθεν, ἄμμες δ' ὂν τὸ μέσσον / νᾶϊ φορήμμεθα συν μελαίναι).
28. They are arranged into a "Golden" verse, in chiastic order, with a carefully studied vowel arrangement: *o-e, a-a, o-e, u-a, o-e.*
29. *TCTIP*, p. 71.

NOTES TO CHAPTER 4

1. "A Few Dont's" (1913), reprinted in *Poets on Poetry*, p. 321.
2. It is Goethe who criticized Horace for "einer furchtbaren Realität, ohne alle eigentliche Poesie, besonders in den Oden." (*Mittheilungen über Goethe*, ed. F. W. Riemer [Berlin, 1841] vol. 2, pp. 643-44).
3. See *Ars Poetica* 1-23, esp. 14-16.

4. "How Does a Poem Mean?" *An Introduction to Literature* (Boston, 1959), p. 870.
5. See 1.9.1-4; 1.11.4-5; 1.25.19-20; 2.9.1-8; 2.10.15-18, and *Epode* 13.1-3 and, conversely, the release from winter in the spring songs (1.4, 4.7, and 4.12).
6. For a discussion of sea-imagery in Horace see E. M. Blaiklock, "The Dying Storm," *Greece and Rome* 6 (1959), pp. 205-10, and G. Nussbaum, "Some Notes on Symbolism in Horace's Lyric Poetry," *Latomus* 24 (1965), esp. pp. 140-43. Nussbaum sees the ship in five odes (1.5, 2.10, 3.2, 3.29, 4.15) as a "ship of life." C. W. Mendell (*Latin Poetry: The New Poets and the Augustans* [New Haven, 1965], pp. 136-37), sees the same in 1.14, the "ship of state" ode—rightly, I think.
7. See 1.35.12; 2.16.7; 2.18.8; 3.1.42; 4.13.13.
8. See 2.18.20-22; 3.1.33-37; 3.24.3-4.
9. See *Satires* 1.8.13; 2.2.132; 2.3.122-23, 142-57; 2.5.45-50, 84-88, and *Epistles* 1.5.13-14 and 2.2.171-77, 191-92.
10. See 2.3.20, 2.14.25 and 4.7.19, and (not contending for the "most beautiful" title) 2.18.6 and 3.24.62.
11. Steele Commager, "The Function of Wine in Horace's Odes," *TAPA* 88 (1957), p. 80. Cf. also Fraenkel on 1.20: "The idea expressed in the words *mea nec Falernae temperant vites* becomes a symbol of Horace's way of life" (*Horace*, p. 216). For an exhaustive survey of Horace's drinking habits, see A. P. McKinlay, "The Wine Element in Horace," *CJ* 42 (1946), pp. 161-68 and 229-36.
12. Kiessling-Heinze, ed., *Horaz* (Berlin, 1960), vol. 1, p. 175.
13. See also 1.36.13-16; 2.3.13-14; 2.11.12-20; 3.15.15-16; 3.19.9-22.
14. See also 1.7.22-23; 1.11.6-7; 1.17.21-22; 1.38.1-8; 2.7.19-26; 3.13.2; 3.14.17-18; 4.11.1-5.
15. See also 1.1.21-22; 1.26.6-8; 2.3.9-12; 4.7.1-4; 4.12.3-4.
16. See also 1.28.25-27; 2.9.1-8; 3.1.25-32; 3.29.33-41 and Epode 13. 1-3.
17. This interpretation runs counter to most explanations of the ode, which associate Pyrrha with the sea. But apart from the implications in the name, the words which describe Pyrrha (*flavam, simplex, aurea, nites*) suggest fire more than water.
18. Steele Commager, *The Odes of Horace* (New Haven, 1962), p. 323.
19. The *musa pedestris* of the Epistles is not unacquainted with

the uses of pattern-of-imagery. Cf. 1.12, which from the first word (*fructibus*) to the last beautiful phrase (*aurea fruges / Italiae pleno defudit Copia cornu*) is filled with cornucopic imagery: *copia . . . in medio positorum . . . herbis . . . urtica . . . agellos/ cultaque . . . annona.* Even the philosophic schools are differentiated on this basis: *seu pisces seu porrum et caepe trucidas.*

NOTES TO CHAPTER 5

1. *Q. Horatii Flacci Carminum Libri* IV (London, 1883 rep. 1959), p. xxiii.
2. In The Fourth Day's Interview of *The Pentameron,* Walter Savage Landor has Boccaccio ask the meaning of the words, and Petrarch answer, "The moment I learn it you shall have it. *Laborat trepidare*! *lympha rivo*! *fugax* too! Fugacity is not the action for hard work, or labour." Boccaccio replies, "Since you cannot help me out, I must give up the conjecture, it seems, while it has cost me only half a century."
3. Assonance and even alliteration between *ph* and *f* are distinct possibilities (cf. *pharetra / fraternaque* 1.21.11;) *Fusce, pharetra* 1.22.4; *Phyllidis flavae* 2.4.14 and *Pholoë fugax* 2.5.17), although there appear to be in Horace many cases of alliteration between *ph* and *p*. See E. H. Sturtevant, *The Pronunciation of Greek and Latin* (Chicago, 1940), p. 157 with note.
4. Further pictorial details are suggested in Collinge, *The Structure of Horace's Odes,* pp. 5-6.
5. For the association of *trepidare* with human living, see the next ode in the corpus, 2.4.23: *trepidavit aetas.*

Part II

NOTES TO CHAPTER 1

1. There may be an Alcaean antecedent: 286 LP bears the marginal paraphrase τὰ τοῦ χειμῶνος . . . διαλύεται. See Denys Page, *Sappho and Alcaeus,* pp. 289-90.
2. There may be a countercurrent as well in the contrast *brevis . . . longam* in line 15: life's span is too short to contain extensive hopes.

3. Compare *viridi nitidum caput* and *virenti canities* (1.9.17).
4. *Nitidum* also suggests "glistening with oil," and may be part of a smaller pattern whereby life and spring are wet (*nitidum, regna vini*), winter and death dry (*siccas*). There are other minor contrasts—life is tender (*tenerum*), death harsh (*acris; graves*); life is a game of chance (*sortiere talis*), victims die according to decree (*poscat agna . . . malit haedo*); life's rhythm is irregular (*alterno pede*), death kicks *in tempo giusto* (*aequo pede*).
5. Recorded in Campbell, *Horace: A New Interpretation*, p. 78.
6. "A Note on Horace 'Odes' 1, 4," *CJ* 47 (1953), p. 262.
7. *The Odes of Horace*, p. 268.
8. "Thought-Sequence in the Ode," *Phoenix* 5 (1951), p. 115.
9. "Sobre Horacio C. 1.4," *Emerita* 15 (1947), pp. 159-60.
10. That lines 9-10 as well as lines 11-12 refer to the ceremonies of Faunus is clear from Calpurnius *Ecl.* 1; Virgil, *Aeneid* 7.81 ff. and Ovid, *Fasti* 4.649 ff.
11. "The Role of Faunus in Horace, *Carmina* 1.4," *TAPA* 92 (1961), pp. 13-19.
12. "Horace, Odes 1.4," *CR* 12 (1962), pp. 5-11.
13. *Horaz*, vol. 1, pp. 25-26.
14. It might be noted that s-sounds predominate at the principal caesurae of *both* long and short lines (*hiems, siccas, stabulis, canis, choros, Nymphis, ardens*) until the center of the poem is reached.
15. Barr, *op. cit.*, neatly establishes February as the proper month for *all* the springtime activities in the ode.

NOTES TO CHAPTER 2

1. *Horaz*, vol. 1, p. 55. Horace uses the meter again in 4.10, a less distinguished but almost equally emphatic eight-line poem whose theme is once more the fleetness of time. The only other ode in the fifth Asclepiad, 1.18, is less impressive in its use of diaeresis, and gives up the attempt in the final line.
2. *The Odes of Horace*, p. 285.
3. Lyce is savage and hard-hearted in 3.10; Neobule has new ideas in 3.12; Sybaris has grown soft and unmanly in 1.8; Rhode is *tempestiva* in 3.19, where Telephus is described as

a flourishing tree; Phyllis is introduced amid leaves of parsley, ivy, and tamarisk in 4.11; Phidyle can make only a modest offering in 3.23; Enipeus is a reproving serenader (ἐνίπτω = vocanti duram) in 3.7; Nearchus is a young master in 3.20. There are further suggestions in "On the Unknown Names in the Odes," appendix I in Wickham's edition (Oxford, 1877), pp. 375-77.

4. Review of Commager, *The Odes of Horace*, in *CP* 58 (1963), p. 182. But Pindar's λευκαῖς is often interpreted "envious" or even "mad."
5. *The Structure of Horace's Odes*, p. 111.
6. *Ibid.*, p. 68.
7. *The Odes of Horace*, p. 274.
8. "The Function of Wine in Horace's Odes," *TAPA* 88 (1957), p. 73, note 12.
9. *The Odes of Horace*, p. 274.
10. N. Rudd, "Patterns in Horatian Lyric," *AJP* 81 (1960), p. 374. I must add that Rudd in no way suggests that Leuconoë means "pure mind."
11. See *Studies in the Odes of Horace* (London, 1884), pp. 113-14.
12. Cf. Lucretius 1.326, Virgil *Aeneid* 5.214 and Pliny *NH* 36.154.
13. See especially Martial 14.103 and 104. The older method of straining through linen, considered inferior in Martial, is already passé in Horace *Satires* 2.4.53-57, where as a mock-serious alternative for those who are *au courant*, Horace suggests sinking the yoke of a pigeon's egg.
14. Commager, *op. cit.* (above, note 8), p. 80.
15. A. O. Hulton ("Horace Odes 1.11.6-7," *CR* 8[1958], pp. 106-7) has demonstrated that *spatio brevi* is not a separate metaphor drawn from the race-course.
16. *Horaz*, vol. 1, p. 175.

NOTES TO CHAPTER 3

1. Lord Lytton, tr., *The Odes and Epodes of Horace* (London, 1872), p. 82.
2. Fraenkel, *Horace*, p. 184.
3. Collinge (*The Structure of Horace's Odes*, p. 68) finds twenty-three odes "of this simple type."
4. J. M. Cordray ("The Structure of Horace's *Odes*: Some

Typical Patterns," *CJ* 52[1956], p. 113 and fn. 5) finds this pattern in eleven of the odes.

5. Commager, *The Odes of Horace,* p. 156.
6. H. J. Rose holds that 1.23 is a variation on Anacreon frag. 88 Diehl (72 P), and that *inuleo* accordingly means mule-colt. See "Some Passages of Latin Poets," *HSCP* 47 (1936), pp. 2-4.
7. The similes form "an amatory commonplace," yet Commager notes that "Horace touches it only to repudiate it" (*op. cit.,* p. 238). *Inuleo . . . similis* suggests Anacreon frag. 39 Diehl (408 P), yet Fraenkel notes "a style far more ornate than is likely to have been employed by Anacreon" (*op. cit.,* p. 183).
8. There is a similar use of the adjective in 3.19.25-27: *tempestiva Rhode* seeks Telephus who is *spissa . . . nitidum coma.*
9. The best explanation is J. G. Orelli (*Q. Horatius Flaccus* [Zürich, 1837, rev. 1868], *ad v.*: *ferae primum cervices cervorum frangunt, deinde eos lacerant*). He cites *Iliad* 11.113 and Valerius Flaccus 2.458.
10. *Horace Odes and Epodes* (Liverpool, 1953) *ad v.*

NOTES TO CHAPTER 4

1. *Carminum Libri* IV, p. 188.
2. *The Pentameron*: Fourth Day's Interview. The sentiments are put in the mouth of Boccaccio, but such emphatic words as "wretched" and "trash" identify the author as the same Landor who wrote marginal comments.
3. "*Romanae Fidicen Lyrae*: The Odes of Horace," in *Critical Essays in Roman Literature,* ed. J. P. Sullivan (London, 1962), p. 196.
4. See W. K. C. Guthrie, *Orpheus and Greek Religion* (London, 1952), pp. 40-41, especially the quotation from Themistius *Or.* 30.349b.
5. Smith Palmer Bovie, *Virgil's Georgics* (Chicago, 1956), p. xxviii.
6. Lines from the descent to Hades in the *Aeneid* (6.306-8) occur unchanged in the Orpheus story in the *Georgics* (4.475-77). If (as many critics, relying on Servius *In Georgicon* 4.1 and *In Bucolicon* 10.1, hold) the Aristaeus-Orpheus epyllion was a later addition to the fourth *Georgic,* these

lines could have been composed for the *Aeneid,* then quoted as a signature to the revised fourth *Georgic.* For bibliography on the subject, see George E. Duckworth, "Recent Work on Virgil," *CW* 57 (1964), p. 204.

7. I have developed this idea at greater length in "Virgil as Orpheus," *Orpheus* 11 (1964), pp. 9-18.
8. Similarly, Page (*op. cit.,* p. 249) notes that Horace "reproduces almost the phraseology" of the third *Georgic* in 2.9, addressed to a poet-friend of his and Virgil's, C. Valgius Rufus.

NOTES TO CHAPTER 5

1. This antiphony is itself the subject of a mild joke. The ode *Ille et nefasto* (2.13) is an elaborate means of proclaiming the Alcaic the best of all possible lyric meters, better even than the Sapphic (cf. lines 29 ff.). Up to this point in Book II, Alcaics (1, 3, 5, 7, 9, 11) and Sapphics (2, 4, 6, 8, 10) had alternated. No. 12, in the third Asclepiad, upset the order. With no. 13, the Alcaic clearly moves into the lead, and maintains it (14, 15, 17, 19, 20—as against Sapphic 16).
2. Cf. Fraenkel: "*εἰρωνεία,* the attitude of a man who is habitually *dissimulator opis propriae,* is here carried to the extreme . . . he is indulging in an enormous understatement." (*Horace,* p. 298)
3. Fraenkel (*op. cit.,* p. 301) calls the detail in the third stanza "repulsive or ridiculous, or both." G. L. Hendrickson ("*Vates Biformis,*" *CP* 44[1949], pp. 30-32) and E. T. Silk ("A Fresh Approach to Horace II, 20," *AJP* 77[1956], pp. 255-63) take Horace seriously. Wilkinson (*HLP,* p. 62) considers the third stanza whimsical but regards the rest as serious. H. Musurillo ("The Poet's Apotheosis: Horace *Odes* 1.1," *TAPA* 93[1962], p. 238) calls the poem "a mock apotheosis."
4. Fraenkel's exclamation is once more "an enormous understatement" (*op. cit.,* p. 304), but this time he sees neither humor nor dissimulation. "Diffident" is from Collinge (see *The Structure of Horace's Odes,* pp. 69-70), who notes that Horace's claims to immortality become less confident as the poem proceeds: "vv. 1-5, I shall outlast all forces of the world and time . . . vv. 6-9, well—I shall last as long as Rome,

in her present form . . . vv. 10-14, well—at least I shall be permanently famous in Apulia." One might add that there are some puzzling expressions best explained as puns (*regali situ, pauper aquae . . . regnavit*); that the basis for Horace's immortality (*princeps Aeolium carmen ad Italos/ deduxisse modos*) is ambiguously stated; that we are left to guess whose merits have won the *superbiam*; that balding Horace ends his Odes with the metrically isolated pyrrhic *comam.*

5. Commager, *The Odes of Horace*, p. 118.
6. *Carminum Libri* IV, p. 219.
7. *Op. cit.*, p. 72.
8. A. W. Verrall, excepting 4, 7, 8, and 12, remarks, "But for these four poems the book might be called a dirge." (*Studies in the Odes of Horace*, p. 8).
9. Cf. *De Rerum Natura* 4.1131 ff.
10. Kiessling-Heinze, *Horaz*, vol. 1, p. 175.
11. Commager, "The Function of Wine in Horace's Odes," *TAPA* 88 (1957), p. 80.
12. There are of course differences in quantity as well as orthography.
13. See "The Pattern of Sound and the Atomistic Theory," *AJP* 62 (1941), pp. 16-34.
14. Cyril Bailey, ed. *De Rerum Natura* (Oxford, 1947), vol. 1, p. 159.
15. It is interesting to note that ten years later Horace ends the fourth book with an ode which begins as another playful excursus on his own art, but ends in graceful obeisance to the memory of Virgil: peace is here, let us spend our days, ferial and festal, with our families, reading the *Aeneid* (4:15.25-32).

NOTES TO CHAPTER 6

1. "Thought-Sequence in the Ode," *Phoenix* 5 (1951), p. 114.
2. This is the suggestion made by Wilkinson, *HLP*, p. 37, fn. 1.
3. Compare *coerces* (1.10.18) and *compulerit* (1.24.18).
4. Commager, *The Odes of Horace*, p. 287.
5. *The Structure of Horace's Odes*, p. 95.
6. *Op. cit.*, p. 285.
7. This pattern has already been noted by C. Dahl, "Liquid Imagery in *Eheu Fugaces*," *CP* 48 (1953), p. 240, who adds

that "Aeolus is a son of Poseidon and is often associated with storms at sea," and by N. Rudd, "Patterns in Horatian Lyric," *AJP* 81 (1960), p. 379, who adds that "Pluto is not merely grim but tearless."

8. See Rudd's additional remarks in *op. cit.*, p. 378.
9. Cf. *Satires* 2.6.18, *Epistles* 1.7.1-9; 1.16.16, and Virgil's *Georgics* 1.311 ff.
10. For the association of the cypress with death, cf. *Epodes* 5.18, Virgil *Aeneid* 6.216, and Ovid *Met.* 10.144 ff. On *brevem dominum,* Heinze (*Horaz,* ad v.) compares the vegetative *breve lilium* (1.36.16), *breves/flores* (2.3.13-14) and *brevis . . . fructus* (Lucretius 3.914).
11. There are, of course, other patterns in 2.14, notably the three emphatic gerundives (as against three future participles in 2.3) *enaviganda . . . visendus . . . linquenda,* and other groups of three: there is no staving off wrinkles, old age, death; we fear war, shipwreck, sickly season; we must look on Cocytus, the Danaids, Sisyphus; we must leave land, home, wife; three hecatombs; thrice-ample Geryon.
12. For the significance of *flavus* see A. W. Verrall, "Quam Tiberis Lavit," in *Studies in the Odes of Horace,* pp. 134-45: "Why is the river golden? Because the banks are of weak sand, and the river is silently 'washing' them away." Verrall cites 3.29.32 ff. as another example, and says that in Augustus' reign floods "occurred with appalling frequency."

NOTES TO CHAPTER 7

1. *Poetics,* chapter 6.
2. Calaïs (topaz) was a son of Boreas and the first youth to inspire homosexual love (see Phanocles, *Erotes* 7-10, the source for Ovid, *Met.* 10.83-85); Thurii was built on the site of Sybaris in southern Italy. Chloë (young shoot) is surrounded by woodland imagery in 1.23; Thrace is proverbially the wildest part of Greece.
3. These finally establish the boy's identity. The volatile, quick-tempered Horace seems to have remembered *levior cortice et improbo / iracundior Hadria* when he described himself in the Epistles as *irasci celerem, tamen ut placabilis essem* (1.20.25).

INDEX OF PROPER NAMES

INDEX OF PASSAGES CITED FROM HORACE